info@kinfolk.com
www.kinfolk.com

Kinfolk Magazine
328 NE Failing Street
Portland, Oregon 97212 USA
Telephone: 503-946-8400
Printed in Canada

Publication Design by Charlotte Heal
Cover Photograph by Neil Bedford

KINFOLK

TOAST

TOA.ST

NATHAN WILLIAMS

Editor in Chief & Creative Director

GEORGIA FRANCES KING

Editor

ANJA VERDUGO

Art Director

GAIL O'HARA

Deputy Editor

CHARLOTTE HEAL

Design Director

DOUG BISCHOFF

Business Operations

KATIE SEARLE-WILLIAMS

Business Manager

NATHAN TICKNOR

Operations Manager

JENNIFER JAMES WRIGHT

Ouur Design Director

JESSICA GRAY

Community Director

PAIGE BISCHOFF

Accounts Payable & Receivable

JESSE HIESTAND

Web Administrator

JOANNA HAN

Contributing Editor

AMANDA JANE JONES

Founding Designer

AMY WOODROFFE

Ouur Editorial Manager

ANDREA SLONECKER

Recipe Editor

KELSEY SNELL

Proofreader

ALICA FORNERET

Editorial Assistant

RACHEL EVA LIM

Editorial Assistant

GAEA CAMPE

Operations Assistant

CHANDLER CORALLO

Business Assistant

SUBSCRIBE
KINFOLK IS PUBLISHED FOUR TIMES A YEAR
TO SUBSCRIBE, VISIT WWW.KINFOLK.COM/SUBSCRIBE OR EMAIL US AT SUBSCRIBE@KINFOLK.COM

CONTACT US
IF YOU HAVE QUESTIONS OR COMMENTS, PLEASE WRITE TO US AT INFO@KINFOLK.COM
FOR ADVERTISING INQUIRIES, GET IN TOUCH AT ADVERTISING@KINFOLK.COM

www.kinfolk.com

MADE & CRAFTED™
LEVI'S®

ISSUE SIXTEEN CONTRIBUTORS

MICHAEL ANTHONY
Writer
New York, New York

SARAH BAIRD
Writer
New Orleans, Louisiana

NEIL BEDFORD
Photographer
London, United Kingdom

JONAS BJERRE-POULSEN
Photographer
Copenhagen, Denmark

PETER BLOCK
Writer
Cincinnati, Ohio

ELLIE VIOLET BRAMLEY
Writer
London, United Kingdom

RODRIGO CARDOSO
Photographer
Lisbon, Portugal

RACHEL CAULFIELD
Stylist
London, United Kingdom

LIZ CLAYTON
Writer
Brooklyn, New York

KATRIN COETZER
Illustrator
Cape Town, South Africa

DANIELLE DEMETRIOU
Writer
Tokyo, Japan

TINA MINAMI DHINGRA
Producer
Tokyo, Japan

TRAVIS ELBOROUGH
Writer
London, United Kingdom

MARGARET EVERTON
Writer
Portland, Oregon

JUSTIN FANTL
Photographer
Los Angeles, California

MAIA FLORE
Photographer
Paris, France

NICOLE FRANZEN
Photographer
Brooklyn, New York

ANNE FULLERTON
Writer
Sydney, Australia

ALICE GAO
Photographer
New York, New York

GENTL & HYERS
Photographers
New York, New York

HIDEAKI HAMADA
Photographer
Osaka, Japan

CHRISTIE HAYDEN
Writer
Baltimore, Maryland

CARL HONORÉ
Writer
London, United Kingdom

STARR HOUT
Writer
Brooklyn, New York

MIKKEL KARSTAD
Writer
Copenhagen, Denmark

STEPHANIE ROSENBAUM KLASSEN
Writer
Sonoma, California

KATHRIN KOSCHITZKI
Photographer
Nuremberg, Germany

CHRISTOPHE LOUIS
Illustrator
Colombes, France

KAREN MORDECHAI
Photographer
Brooklyn, New York

MIKKEL MORTENSEN
Photographer
Copenhagen, Denmark

MICHAEL NOLLEDO
Writer
Chicago, Illinois

TEC PETAJA
Photographer
Nashville, Tennessee

JULIE POINTER
Writer
Portland, Oregon

LENE RØNFELDT
Stylist
Aarhus, Denmark

SIDSEL RUDOLPH
Stylist
Copenhagen, Denmark

ANDERS SCHØNNEMANN
Photographer
Copenhagen, Denmark

NATHALIE SCHWER
Stylist
Copenhagen, Denmark

ANNU SUBRAMANIAN
Writer
New York, New York

MARTYN THOMPSON
Photographer
New York, New York

JAN VERLINDE
Photographer
Antwerp, Belgium

CHIDY WAYNE
Illustrator
Barcelona, Spain

WICHMANN + BENDTSEN
Photographers
Copenhagen, Denmark

Photo: Romain Bernardie James

www.lapaz.pt

LA PAZ

STUTTERHEIM

RAINCOATS

SWEDISH MELANCHOLY AT ITS DRIEST

WELCOME

Deciding what is essential in our lives isn't about paring back our belongings and forgoing our beloved but unnecessary frivolities: Instead of determining how little we can live with, it's about working out what we simply can't live without.

In the springtime we shed everything except the bare necessities and enter summer wanting to celebrate life's simplest elements: the sun, watermelons, bathing suits, aimless conversations, long books and even longer afternoons. The Essentials Issue of *Kinfolk* will explore the different meanings of life's fundamentals and suggest ways we can incorporate them into our daily lives. We want to uncover the heart, the kernel, the foundation, the bedrock—whatever brings us back to our cores.

While the term *essentialism* often brings to mind an empty wardrobe containing only white cotton T-shirts, we can still invite slowness and simplicity into our days without having to live minimally or tediously. Although essentialism is commonly applied to possessions in our closets, as best-selling author Greg McKeown puts it in an interview on page 98, "We're talking about the closets of our lives."

The concept of our tangible belongings versus our esoteric feeling of belonging is studied in this issue's excerpt from *Community: The Structure of Belonging* by Peter Block. Although we may consider the basic requirements for life to be food, water and shelter, Peter explores the deep-seated desire we have to belong to something larger than ourselves, and suggests ways we can connect our communities to foster genuine support. This togetherness is reflected in other articles in this issue, such as our feature on Tokyo's Yanaka neighborhood, which provides a brief respite to the city's hectic pace.

There are stories about the civil fabric that holds society together, the scientific importance of laughter and the Cloud Appreciation Society's desire for us to look up. Carl Honoré, the author of last issue's excerpt, *In Praise of Slowness*, teaches us the positive side of saying no. Four writers look at the art of conversation and delve into its core components—language, tone, silence and listening—and we interview a series of entrepreneurs from differing creative fields about how they weave essentialism into their practices.

When it comes to food, we make the most of an entire watermelon in a series of recipes with the quintessential summer fruit and cast aside utensils to eat with our hands. The olive groves of Italy provide us with some fertile ground to learn more about the crucial pantry staple of olive oil, and we also reinvent the most basic of pairings: bread and butter.

Of course, something can be said for living frugally—the focused attention, the lack of mental and physical clutter—but a life without joy-bringing superfluous additions isn't really being lived to its potential. So swap your sleep for rambling late-night exchanges. Languish in the bath a little longer. Drink that gin gimlet. Order that second serving of crab cakes. Be thankful for the opportunities you have to indulge in being wholly yourself, and start looking at life through an essentialist lens.

NATHAN WILLIAMS AND GEORGIA FRANCES KING

Community

Food, water and shelter are often touted as the three basic tenets of survival, but our desire to belong to something larger than ourselves is just as important to our happiness in the long run.

Home

A house that's refined to its essence doesn't need to be stark white or empty: Instead of focusing on crafting a minimal home, fill it with warmth, love and everything that matters to you and you alone.

Work

Nothing is more in need of stripping down to the fundamentals than our hectic work lives. Figuring out how to make a living while also staying sane is one of the secrets of a healthy work life.

Play

Our summer activities are highlighted by their lack of additional gear or preparation: Cloud-gazing and wave-watching require nothing more than a free hour and a little patience.

Food

No matter what cuisine we're gathering around a table to eat, food is at the center of many of our cultural traditions. Sometimes it's best to remove a few fancy elements to let the main ingredient shine.

Starters

WORDS
MARGARET EVERTON

The Essential Non-Essentials

The heart of essentialism isn't about asking how little we can live with, but determining what we simply cannot live without.

Like its austere doppelgänger minimalism, essentialism dislikes excess. But you don't have to wear only black, drink coffee without cream or purge your secondhand books to hone life to a fine point. Although living sparely has its virtues, the grand task of essential living is to uncover the elements that bring us rapture.

The thing that encumbers one person is often the buoyant must-have of another. If you search online for "things people can't live without," you'll find lists including anything from a morning cup of coffee to punctuation and a good cry every now and then. We've all witnessed the caprices of another: A friend of mine can't go a day without drinking a shot of melting chocolate, and another never travels without his pillow, stuffing the goose-down rectangle into even the smallest luggage. A digital artist may go home to no screens but 56 houseplants, while a nomad writer constantly relocates with only a large duffel filled with rare books.

What might seem to be eccentricity is actually fine-tuned discipline. Arbitrarily inviting everything that appeals to you into your life is just imprudent excess, like a good dinner party gone haywire because the host didn't bother revising the guest list. Without the guiding discrimination of our inner voices, our lives can be filled randomly with things that may be generally good, but not the best.

A cultivated selectivity can transform plain objects into relics of our life story. Our personal relationship to items gives them significance, an essence that goes beyond their physical properties. Perhaps the ratty paper in our wallet is actually a scrap from a once-visited abbey in Ireland, a reminder to always adventure. Or the random accumulation of hand lotions at our desk is more about our attention to self-care than a product fetish. We might keep an item out of sentiment, to better equip us for life or simply because we just like having it around. Whatever our motivations, this often illogical but honest act of curation humanizes our existence.

Even the questionable habits we can't seem to break help to refine our individuality. Maybe we take conference calls in the bathtub or bust out the bad jokes when we're nervous. The freak flags we may disregard or be embarrassed about might not exactly be virtues in and of themselves, but they're vital elements that make us who we are. Oscar Wilde walked his pet lobster on a leash, Flannery O'Connor doted on her 50 peacocks and the German writer Friedrich Schiller could only work with rotten apples piled in his desk drawer. Friedrich Nietzsche always ignored lunch invitations and instead dined alone on beefsteak and fruit in the middle of a crowded restaurant. He was convinced that the sometimes lonely and awkward struggle to not just be one of the tribe is a worthy price to pay for owning yourself.

Perhaps the entire point of essentialism is this process of self-actualization. If asked to identify the non-negotiables in our lives, we probably wouldn't think about the restraints of our five-item wardrobe or our abstinence from sugar, but about the times when we've palpably lived. We couldn't imagine life without the tribal rug we bought in Tangier or dad's smoking jacket in the back of our closet, unworn but revered. As we follow those internal pulls and sometimes irrational desires, the superfluity disappears and leaves us each with our own messy and eccentric authenticity. And nothing is more essential than that.

PHOTOGRAPH: MIKKEL MORTENSEN; STYLING: LENE RØNFELDT

The Cloud Appreciation Society

*There's no need to head to a far-flung beach
or a cabin in the woods to disconnect:
You just need to look up.*

When it comes to celestial phenomena, clouds have a reputation for being the surly, temperamental cousin no one wants to sit near at Christmas. We rarely notice them, but if we do, it's usually just because they're causing trouble. As both a Londoner and the founder of the Cloud Appreciation Society, Gavin Pretor-Pinney knows this better than most. Over the past decade, Gavin's mission to rebrand clouds has led to three best-selling books, a BBC program, a TED Talk that's been viewed more than a million times and the formation of an online community of at least 37,000 cloud lovers. Here, we chat with him about why clouds are so maligned and what we can learn from the underdog of the skies.

WHEN DID YOU FIRST BECOME FASCINATED WITH CLOUDS?

While being driven to school by my mother at about the age of four, I looked out of the window and saw rays of sunlight bursting out from behind a big puffy cloud. I thought, maybe for the first time, "I wonder what that is? What's it made of, why is it up there and what would it be like to sit on?" As I got older, I became curious about why people in Britain complain about them so much. We even have negative connotations written into the language: We talk about depressed people "having a dark cloud hanging over them" and there being "clouds on the horizon." I've always felt that they get unfair press, and it seems to me that we should stand up for them. I realized later in life that that someone should be me.

WHY DO WE NEED A CLOUD APPRECIATION SOCIETY?

If you just shift your perspective slightly on this ever-present backdrop to our lives, it's easy to see the beautiful, the surprising, the exotic in the everyday mundane stuff around you. Cloud-spotting is kind of meditating on nature, and the sky is a very egalitarian part of that. You don't need to live in an area of outstanding beauty to look up at outstandingly beautiful skies—you could live in an inner-city urban environment where the sky is the last wilderness visible to you. The valuable aspect is that it's easy to engage with.

WHAT ARE SOME OF THE BENEFITS OF CLOUD-SPOTTING?

It's good for creative thought because it allows the other modes of the brain to kick in. When you let your mind wander, you begin to make creative connections. It's also good for your soul and health to be able to disengage from the ever-present to-do list. Layered on top of all the traditional pressures of our lives, we now have all the pressures of the digital world, which has this effect of making us feel as if we should be doing something all the time. One of the values of cloud-spotting is that it legitimizes doing nothing.

HOW HAS CLOUD-SPOTTING HELPED YOU?

Those struggles are as apparent to me as they are for anyone. Staring at clouds helps me disentangle myself. I'm quite goal-focused, and the clouds help remind me of the value of the process. They are forever in process, forever in change. To engage with them is not to be focused on an endpoint. In fact, that's one reason why I don't take photographs of clouds these days: I find it's more valuable to see a beautiful cloudscape, value it and then let it go.

DO YOU HAVE A CLOUD-SPOTTING ROUTINE?

I don't. It's a bit like when someone asks, "Where's the best place to watch clouds?" Being a cloud spotter is an attitude. It's a matter of being prepared to pause for a moment and stop whatever is pressing right now when you notice something interesting in the sky. I have two daughters who are 5 and 8 and if one of them says "Dad, look at the sun," it's easy to say, "Yes, I've just got to send this email first." There's always something to stop you stepping back. It's not about having a routine—it's just about being prepared to stop what seems urgent right now and enjoy the moment.

WORDS
LIZ CLAYTON

Keeping it Civil

Our lives are dictated by unspoken rules that keep society moving smoothly and civilly. Without them, imagine the impolite chaos that would descend.

Human beings are nicer than you may think. This is hard to imagine on tough days of course and especially in big cities: that person taking up too much room on the train, that parent letting a gaggle of children scream at top volume when you just can't deal, that jerk stealing your cab. But what about all the other times we've secretly, quietly agreed to support each other, even lift each other up, and co-woven the fabric of mutual preservation by simply participating in a silent code of being civilized?

Despite its rough and rude reputation, New York City is a fine example of the hidden warmth and order beneath the everyday. Don't believe it? Try walking down a sidewalk without an umbrella on a pouring day: You'll be stopped on the street, you'll be worried about and, in extremely rainy circumstances, you may be offered an umbrella. These offers come from the please-and-thank-you set, the seat-offerers and the help-your-stroller-up-the-stairs folks, who are everywhere, believe it or not.

These aren't habits learned from motivational subway posters or after-school specials: This is the socially supportive order we learn by watching each other. It's the instinct that brings an extra napkin to the table for you or lets your car slip into busy traffic, a dance of manners we're all teaching one another every day.

Our parents often get us started on this road: You say "excuse me" when you get up from the table, walk to the right so that others may pass and help the elderly across the street. But what we all do for each other, as part of that continuing social education, is teach by way of example. When someone on a bus or train near you offers a seat to another who needs it more, it snaps you out of your reverie. "Why didn't I see that person?" you ask yourself, which can lead to "What do others need that I can give?"

Where I live, we say hello to others we meet in the street not to start conversations, but to remind each other of our human-ness. Like two dogs meeting, all that's needed is a simple tail-wag to get the point across: *I'm friendly. You're friendly. I see you.* It's amazing how far this simple act of acknowledgment can go in turning tough terrain into a place that feels like home, where you'll truly see the humans around you and your next move will be another act of sharing space and kindness.

There are written codes of moral conduct too, such as signs telling you to obey traffic laws, to not dump your beer cans in the river and to not stand on the edges of high-up slippery things. Many of these social commandments exist because you may either get hurt or may hurt others if you don't obey. But there are also signs that tell you to not sit on the grass, or to not slip quietly behind chained-off waterfront vistas, where there's no high wind or harm done, and where someone else's mandate is masquerading as morality. Take these rare chances when no one else is getting hurt to live freely and sneak past that rope. Have that first kiss with someone special, hidden in darkness along a backlit city skyline, and pay forward the richness of your experience by continuing to look for ways to be kind to others and live fully within your environment.

ILLUSTRATIONS: KATRIN COETZER

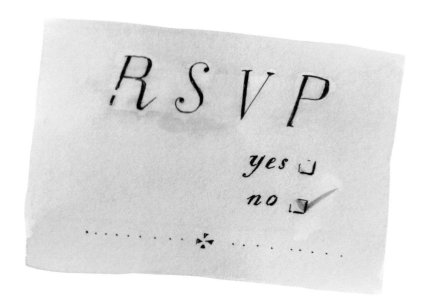

WORDS
CARL HONORÉ

The Positive Side of Negatives

One of the world's most respected advocates of the Slow movement explains why we should all say no more often.

Elton John was wrong when he sang that *sorry* seems to be the hardest word. No—nowadays the hardest word is, uh, *no*.

Think about it. There's a reason the villain from the first James Bond film wasn't called *Dr. Yes*: Nobody likes saying no, either to themselves or to others.

That's because saying no is hard to do. It smacks of puritanical party pooping, which goes against the grain in a permissive, post-boomer world where everyone wants to have it all. Coined during the war on drugs, one of the most joyless slogans of recent times has to be: Just Say No. Nobody likes to miss out on stuff or let others down.

Even when we yearn to give the thumbs down, those around us can make it hard to do. Children know exactly what buttons to push to elicit a yes from parents who are desperate to keep the peace. What's more, the world is now full of graduates of assertiveness-training courses who proudly "refuse to take no for an answer." But this is folly: Sometimes the smartest thing to do *is* to make no your answer.

Yet changes in the job market have made the word no even less palatable. More of us are now self-employed, and the first rule of Freelance Club is never turn down work, ever. In fact, a consultant friend of mine has a dubious motto: "Say *yes yes yes* to everything, and then figure out later how to cram it all in."

Delivering a smiling yes to everyone may seem polite, but it can cause more offense in the long run. Many of us accept invitations and then fail to show up because we're too tired or overbooked. One way to avoid that kind of rudeness is to be honest with people—and yourself—and RSVP graciously with a no up front. Besides, saying yes to everything can strap you to a hamster wheel where there is never enough time to think, listen, rest, dream, savor or connect with other people. You'll end up racing through life instead of living it.

Resisting the pressure to say yes brings other benefits too. It keeps you from being a doormat. It lightens your schedule so you can focus on the stuff that really matters. Hearing no more often might also make us less selfish, less inclined to expect the world to indulge our every whim. And the more you hear no, the sweeter yes sounds.

The bottom line is that one of the secrets of life is knowing when to say yea and when to say nay, to pinpoint what is essential and let the rest fall by the wayside. A good place to start is to pause, look at the big picture and reflect on what really counts. That way you can weed out the stuff that only *seems* essential, and then chuck it in the no trash can.

Let's give the final word to one of the masters of the business universe. When asked for advice on how to stay ahead of the pack, the billionaire Warren Buffett made it clear that less yes is more: "The difference between successful people and very successful people," he quipped, "is that very successful people say no to almost everything."

Kinfolk's take on Starr's bedside table: Bella Coffee Table by HAY in oak. Piani Table Lamp by Ronan & Erwan Bouroullec for Flos in white. Shirt by Zara. Bedspread and glassware by HAY. Books by Samuel Beckett, Simone de Beauvoir and Michael Elmgreen & Ingar Dragset.

My Bedside Table:
The Fashion Designer

*Starr Hout, who cofounded the New York–based
fashion brand Apiece Apart with her friend
Laura Cramer, talks about her evening rituals
and how she's made her bedroom kid-friendly.*

There's nothing in my bedroom except a bed, a crib and two side tables. I consider it a sanctuary and sacred space. I like to keep work away from my bed, which means no notebooks, sketchpads or pens. I've learned to keep my phone away from my sleeping area too— preferably in the other room, which helps us all sleep through the night. This really helps with putting my mind at ease and ensures that I'm not checking my notifications or responding to messages just before I go to bed. I like to shower before bed in order to wash the day away, then I try to feel grounded through stillness and meditation, which usually calms my nerves for a solid slumber.

It's pretty important for me to have a bedside table with sufficient space to put various objects, so smaller tables just won't do. I chose a nightstand that's roughly the same height as my bed, which maintains the plane and makes it easy to retrieve things: It's a Tablo tray table designed by Magnus Löfgren, complete with an Anglepoise lamp and a Braun clock.

A couple of the objects that live on my bedside table are some Aesop hand cream and a meditation singing bowl that doubles as a toy for my little 11-month-old, Finn, who's drawn to its shiny brass and its ability to make music. While we've had to make some changes in our nighttime routines to adapt to a baby's unpredictable sleep cycle, it's been a joy changing the bedroom to suit his needs and sharing our space with him. Unfortunately, flowers are too much of a distraction for Finn though, as he loves to touch and often destroy bouquets.

In the morning I'm a firm devotee of Grady's Coffee in a Robert Blue mug, and in the evening I'm never without a jumbo-size canning jar of water with a spike of coconut water. I don't snack in bed all that much as it gets too messy, and I like a really clean bed.

When it comes to sleepwear, I favor Apiece Apart's Peruvian tees or slip dresses, and I adore my white Fog Linen pillowcases and French linen bed sheets from Le Monde Sauvage in Paris. I'm a big fan of white beds and pieces of furniture that are simple, functional and timeless in their beauty. I love the blonde wood, burlap curtains, white linen sheets and sheepskin elements of my bedroom.

I enjoy reading soft, feel-good books before hitting the sack. Some of the ones currently on the table are *The Art of Stillness* by Pico Iyer, *The Everlasting Meal* by Tamar Adler and the poetry of Mary Oliver. Before drifting off to sleep, or sometimes in dreams, my mind often returns to my favorite places in nature or sees light sparkling through the leaves and dancing on the sea.

While I'm usually an early riser, I end up spending a lot of time in bed throughout the day thanks to Finn's nursing schedule. There's a large tree right in front of our apartment that I love to look at while I'm nursing. I find its wide, generous arms inspiring, refreshing and recharging.

COMPILED BY
ALICA FORNERET

Culinary Essentials

We asked some of our favorite chefs and food intensives what they've learned about life from years in the kitchen.

NICK KORBEE, EGG SHOP, NEW YORK CITY:

I've learned to brine, season or marinate lean meats well in advance, and it's a dirty old French trick, but finishing with butter goes a long way. In terms of lessons that the kitchen has taught me about my nonculinary life, there have been a few standouts: You'll be judged on what you promise and fail to deliver; caring for your mental health and physical well-being isn't a sign of weakness; the loudest voice will never be heard; and keep your mouth shut until it's a sure thing, and even then never ever brag or boast. You should also cook to make someone other than yourself happy: When I'm cooking, I'm often thinking of specific people in my life, usually my wife or my late Grandma Betty. If it's something I'd be very excited to serve them, chances are I've given it my all.

KRISTEN MURRAY, MAURICE, PORTLAND, OREGON:

Keep it simple and honor the ingredients. There should be no more than three components, and layer the natural essence of the star ingredient. For example, I can make my great-aunt's candied kumquats from memory. They're sheer heaven! I always have them in my pantry. I'd crawl up her jacaranda tree, eat as many kumquats as I could until my stomach ached and only then would I fill up the front of her apron like a kangaroo pouch and bring the fruit to her. I've learned that a strong leader goes much farther than an egotistical mentor. There's always a way—thinking and pushing beyond the known always proves for greater flexibility and function in life.

JUSTIN BURKE-SAMSON, PARTY OF TWO, BOSTON, MASSACHUSETTS:

Keep things clean! I've had to learn this the hard way. I operate in a mode that my mother calls "controlled chaos." An outsider might think I'm out of control, but internally I know exactly where everything is. I didn't think much of it until I realized that cooking is so much better if you keep the process clean. I've learned to roll with the punches, to not be so damn serious and to think creatively when faced with a challenge in my every day. In the kitchen you're always putting out little fires, so if something doesn't go as planned or it's just an off day, it happens and that's OK.

DANIEL ESPINOZA, DINNER LAB, NEW ORLEANS, LOUISIANA:

I know they're not very essential, but my pantry is never complete without tortillas, Fruit Loops and whiskey! If I've learned anything, it's whatever you do, do it right and do it with love. Cooking is all about love and patience. One recipe I love is *chilaquiles*, without a doubt. Every Saturday morning my mom would make red chilaquiles—I'd hear the Spanish onions sizzling on the cast-iron pan like an alarm clock. Mom would vigorously stir the pan, add the tortillas that were probably stale, then we'd hear the sharp noise of deglazing as the *salsa roja* hit the hot pan with ripples of hot oil and sauce clashing with each other. The temperature would drop to a simmer and, as soon as the tortillas absorbed the salsa, mom would make it rain with *queso fresco*. She'd yell our names, and it would be served as soon as we walked in the kitchen.

JESSICA KOSLOW, SQIRL, LOS ANGELES, CALIFORNIA:

I've discovered that if you season as you go, it ensures that each layer is just right. When you work with good ingredients, it doesn't take much to make them sing. Some key ingredients in my kitchen are fresh mint, French *sel gris* and preserved lemons, but I couldn't live without popcorn, ice cream and wine. With any ingredient or recipe, you should feel free to improvise as you go. The more you take those risks, the more you can learn to trust yourself and where your palate tells you to go.

IGNACIO MATTOS, ESTELA, NEW YORK CITY:

Food should be bold, clean, delicious and simple. Editing is extremely important to make that happen and to develop our language in the kitchen. When we started out, we would take things away at the end of the process. Now we continue to learn, but we're able to edit before things go on the plate. You have to trust your palate and know the parameters you're working with. You have to be confident. But you also have to be restless and critical of yourself. Part of that is having everybody on the staff try the food and give opinions and create a common language.

LAURYN CHUN, THE KIMCHI COOKBOOK, NEW YORK CITY:

Creating good backbones of flavor to achieve umami in a dish is essential: Adding a bit of dried dashi or anchovy paste to my tomato sauce gives extra umami back notes.

QUEALY WATSON, HOT JOY, SAN ANTONIO, TEXAS:

Aside from my pressure cooker and smoker, fish sauce is one of the vital items in my kitchen: I put a dash in almost everything to provide salt and an umami flavor. It works great as a main component in dressings and seasoning clam chowder, and it's my go-to steak sauce when you deglaze a pan after cooking a steak in brown butter with a little lemon juice. I've learned that work is great when you love what you do, but if you ignore life, you'll find it gone when you look up. Relax, take your time, enjoy the therapy of crafting something personal to share. And there's always a moment of learning in failure, so pull the batteries out of the smoke alarm before you start cooking.

JOSHUA MCFADDEN, AVA GENE'S, PORTLAND, OREGON:

Keep clean, stay organized and plan ahead. If you're having a party, what can you do ahead of time? Set up a workstation and have all the things you need in front of and around you. Some of the items I keep readily available in my larder are Parmesan cheese, garlic, dried chilies and lemons.

GONTRAN CHERRIER, GONTRAN CHERRIER BOULANGER, PARIS:

I've learned that we can always get better, improve our techniques and should never take anything for granted. We should take the time to enjoy what we're doing and, even more importantly, to always please the people we're serving. And that means precise serving sizes, precise cooking time, a hint of greed and some creativity.

WORDS
MICHAEL NOLLEDO

Passeggiata

Taking a destination-less meander as the sun sets is a common mind-clearing ritual in Italian culture.

LANGUAGE: Italian
PRONUNCIATION: "pah-say-jah-tah"
ETYMOLOGY: Derived from *passeggiare*: to take steps, pass through
MEANING: To take a *passeggiata* is to master the art of an evening stroll. It's a means to walk aimlessly and enjoy the simple pleasure of being outdoors and socializing in the lingering summer sun. Those of us who move too fast to take in the day's offerings might consider the Italians' mindful meandering pace troubling, but the longer the stride the more relaxed the conversation. This ritual is a reflection of community, of shared glances across busy piazzas, of families with new strollers, young lovers who still have much to learn of grace and well-dressed elderly folks with their hands folded behind their backs. It's street-side theater and feels a lot like a collective pursuit, even when taken alone.
USE: The ideal time to take a passeggiata is between late afternoon and dusk as a break between finishing work and sitting down to dinner. Try organizing a passeggiata instead of indoor happy-hour beverages: It's a moving meeting place for family and friends where you can report on the day's events and rest before the evening ahead.

WORDS
ALICA FORNERET

Hands-on Advantage

Eating with your hands is a playful way to reconnect with your food, your friends and your taste buds.

When the sun hangs in the sky past 9 P.M. and the scent of barbecue coals fills the air, it's clear that summer has arrived. Items that were considered necessities in winter are retired, such as the shoes that deny our toes the sensory pleasure of sand-shuffling and the weekly planners we trade for books as deadlines fade. One of the best summer adaptions is eating with our hands in favor of utensils: Grabbing a hot dog on a coastal boardwalk frees a hand for holding someone else's, and both county fair food and ice creams conveniently come on a stick. Abandoning eating tools isn't only convenient, it allows us to use the utensils we were born with to foster a deeper relationship with our picnic snacks and campfire fare.

Physiologically, our hands are organs of action. From the first moment we touch our food, the nerve endings in our fingers fire signals to our brain, telling us when and how to interact with a meal. Picking up a piece of food lets the brain decide if it's too hot to put in our mouths, and forming bites with our fingers also prepares our stomachs for the oncoming food, as our bodies' cephalic phase gets the digestive juices flowing whenever we touch, taste, smell or even think about food. Combining forces with our senses, our hands can be a vital tool used to foster a well-rounded tactile experience with our meal, which can be lost when chopsticks or a fork—which are arguably unnecessary middlemen to our dining experiences—are involved.

In addition to the physical benefits, the practice can also shape how we look at the act of eating and sharing meals with our communities. Some cultures even see the absence of utensils as an opportunity to explore the deep connection between people and food. Ethiopian restaurateur Fetlework Tefferi once noted that "We need to revisit the way people used to eat: They cared and believed that whatever they put into their mouths was sacred." In Ethiopia, *goorsha* is an act of friendship and love that involves directly feeding someone sharing a meal with you. Using your hands to shape a bite of food and putting it in someone else's mouth shows respect, care and affection. "Eating with the hands is more than just a mechanism to get sustenance into the mouth," she said.

The warm season is a perfect time to exercise this hand-to-mouth practice: Ribs would be infinitely less enjoyable if we couldn't lick the sauce that covers our palms, and stone fruit juices leave sticky memories well after our noshing. But we can consider any meal as an opportunity to enrich our relationship with food both physically and mentally. So whether you're enjoying takeout on an outdoor movie date or eating potato salad on the Fourth of July, ditch the fork and dig in hands first.

WORDS
TRAVIS ELBOROUGH

Simple Philosophies

*But what does it all mean?
Many great philosophical minds have
tried to pare down their theorems
to find the fundamental truths.*

Often when we think about philosophy, we think about big ideas, complicated theories and untamable beards. While browsing the 900 pages of Immanuel Kant's *Critique of Pure Reason*, who hasn't thought they could do with, well, less? Less of it for a start—and perhaps less of philosophy generally. Yet since the classical times, philosophy has been fundamentally concerned with getting at the essential truths to the messy questions of life, the universe and basically everything. For all the long words and big books, thinkers have simply been trying to help us to live better lives.

Turning first to the Ancient Greeks, we come across Socrates, the father of the quizzical Socratic method of inquiry and star of *Bill & Ted's Excellent Adventure*. This great Athenian proposed giving up material goods, arguing that we can only be truly happy by freeing ourselves from hankering after wealth and status. Anyone who was "not contented with what they had would not be contented with what they would like to have," he reasoned.

Epicurus—another Greek philosopher—held that pleasure was the highest good. He promoted a doctrine called Hedonism that many still associate with the earthly excesses that Socrates frowned on. Dictionaries commonly define an Epicurean as "a devotee of sensuous and luxurious living." But thrill-seeking visitors to Epicurus's school just outside of Athens were shocked to find a man who drank only water, dined ascetically on vegetables and regarded "a pot of cheese" as a feast. For Epicurus, pleasure was living well. And to live well, one had to be healthy and free from hunger and pain. Since indulging one's appetite to excess could lead to sickness, emotional distress and reduce the overall quality of life, he believed it should be avoided. He therefore suggested that a plain but nourishing meal of nuts and berries could offer more intrinsic pleasure than a lavish banquet. To his mind, what constituted "abundance" was "not what we *have* but what we *enjoy*." Like Socrates, he argued that for anyone who thought that "enough" was too little, then nothing would ever be quite enough. Epicurus's ideas were embraced by the so-called Stoics, who counseled frugal, reclusive living and acceptance of suffering, and counted the Roman thinker Seneca as one of their leading lights, despite dining lavishly himself.

In the Middle Ages, William of Ockham, a Franciscan who had taken vows of poverty and chastity, became the next major apostle of philosophical simplicity. He urged thinkers not to "multiply entities beyond their necessity"—in other words, keep things simple, guys. When faced with two competing theories, he believed that the simpler one would usually prove best. This principle became known as Occam's razor and remains an invaluable tool for eliminating metaphysical waste.

But Western philosophy's most audacious attempt to strip things right back to basics perhaps comes from René Descartes, who decided to "demolish everything completely and start again from the foundations" while holed up in a Bavarian farmhouse in the bitter winter of 1619. By questioning all of his beliefs about the world, he concluded that the only thing he could not doubt was that he was thinking. From this, he derived his famous maxim, "I think, therefore I am."

Naturally, philosophers have been arguing about this ever since. But then again, as Confucius once observed, "Life is really simple, but we insist on making it complicated."

WORDS
CHRISTIE HAYDEN

Ode to Bread and Butter

The simple beauty of this classic pairing shouldn't be confined to side plates: Turn to the following pages for some spruced-up recipes.

Oh, bread and butter, you are more than just an appetizer—you're the sustenance of a global population and the pivotal point in a meal.

As you disappear as a complimentary offering from so many restaurants, we're here to applaud what may be your final bow. You appear to be fading into a mere dining formality, which is a travesty comparable to art without Pollock's paradoxical precision or film without Godard's breaking of the fourth wall.

As gluten naysayers banish you from tabletops, we find ourselves longing for images of elegant French women with baguettes tucked under their arms as they strut down the Champs-Élysées. We imagine jovial times spent singing the praises of hot cross buns while images of Easter pastries with buttery icing float freely through our minds.

Butter, you are salted when feeling bold and unsalted in your more languid state. Bread, you are an old soul, but nevertheless quite the cultural chameleon: We appreciate the full breadth of your character, whether it's focaccia, pumpernickel, challah, *injera*, tortillas or naan. Together, you eclipse other notable twosomes: Lewis and Clark, Tom and Huck, F. Scott and Zelda, hydrogen and oxygen.

While you are now denigrated to a mere side order, we shall never forget your previous prominence. Bread and butter, you will forever be our figurative bread and butter.

WORDS
STEPHANIE ROSENBAUM KLASSEN

Human Resources

Have you ever forgotten the basic tools for opening your drink in the woods? It's amazing what we're capable of when thirsty.

Out in the wilderness, ingenuity can save the day. And when we say "wilderness," we mean "lake cabin." And when we say "ingenuity," we mean "opening a bottle of wine with a lace-up shoe."

When stranded far from civilization and YouTube while holding a bottle of Cabernet in one hand and no corkscrew in the other, we start to lose our calm, masterful grip on the living of life. We long to be the one who can pick up some overlooked household instruments —a butter knife, a set of keys—and get that bottle open.

Because let's face it: We forget things. We make the blithe assumption that of course the summer rental will have a corkscrew, can opener and coffee grinder, and we injure our palms trying to pop off what we were sure were twist-top caps back in the store. But regret fills no glasses and blame pops no corks, so here are some quick hacks when you need to be resourceful:

WINE:
The easiest way to a glass of wine is through a twist-off top (or, as we've all resorted to on some occasion, a box). But if a cork is the only obstacle between you and a cool glass on the deck, try these methods:

First, loosen the cork by working a small, sharp blade into the area between it and the neck of the bottle. Act as if you're freeing a cake from a baking pan by jabbing gently up and down in a circle all the way around the cork. Once the cork has been loosened, push it into the bottle with the handle of a table knife or wooden spoon.

Or if you're desperate (and there's an ER nearby), stick the bottom of the bottle firmly into a sturdy, hard-soled shoe. Directing the bottle at a 45-degree angle with the cork facing up, hold the bottle in one hand and the shoe in the other as you tap it firmly against a hard surface such as a flat rock or a concrete wall until the cork inches its way out of the bottle via pressure.

BEER:
There's no need to let that lovely six-pack go to waste just because there's no bottle opener in your picnic basket.

If you don't have a lighter or hands of steel, wiggle the tip of a key under the ridges of the bottle cap and push upward and twist until you've splayed out several ridges. Repeat and slowly work the key tip into the opening you've made and push up to force off the cap.

And remember: You can keep any bottle cold by wrapping it in several layers of damp newspaper.

The Lunch Box: Bread and Butter

This dynamic duo doesn't need to be bland: Keeping some flavored butters on hand can turn any midday snack into a deluxe desk picnic.

ROASTED TOMATO BUTTER

2 cups (280 grams) cherry tomatoes

1 cup (2 sticks/225 grams) unsalted butter, cubed and softened

1 cup (20 grams) fresh cilantro leaves

1½ teaspoons fine sea salt

¼ teaspoon smoked paprika

1 ½ teaspoons fresh lime juice

Makes about 1 ¾ cups (375 grams)

Broil the tomatoes on a small rimmed baking pan lined with aluminum foil until wilted, burst and blistered, turning once, about 10 minutes. Cool to room temperature.

Puree the tomatoes in a food processor until relatively smooth. Add the butter, cilantro, salt and paprika and process to combine. Stop the machine occasionally to scrape down the sides of the bowl and stir the mixture to help it come together. Add the lime juice and process to just incorporate. Taste and adjust the seasoning, adding more salt, paprika or lime juice as desired.

SERVING IDEAS: Roll into warm corn tortillas with chopped cucumber and avocado, use in tea sandwiches with thinly sliced radishes and a handful of watercress, eat on crostini with a slice of roasted red bell pepper and topped with flaked tuna, or try spreading on the outside of the bread before cooking to make the best grilled cheese ever.

STRAWBERRY-BALSAMIC BUTTER

1 cup (2 sticks/225 grams) unsalted butter, cubed and softened

2 cups (275 grams) fresh strawberries, sliced

1 tablespoon sugar

½ cup (10 grams) fresh basil leaves, torn

1 teaspoon very coarsely ground black pepper

1 teaspoon fine sea salt

1 tablespoon plus 2 teaspoons balsamic vinegar

Makes about 1 ¾ cups (375 grams)

Heat a medium sauté pan over medium-high heat. When hot, add 1 tablespoon of the butter and swirl to melt. Add the strawberries and sugar and sauté until most of the berries lose their shape and the juices begin to caramelize, 6 to 8 minutes. Add 1 tablespoon of the balsamic vinegar and continue cooking about 2 minutes more. Remove from the heat and cool to room temperature.

Puree the strawberries in a food processor until relatively smooth. Add the remaining butter, the basil, pepper and salt and process to combine. Stop the machine occasionally to scrape down the sides of the bowl and stir the mixture to help it come together. Add the remaining balsamic vinegar and process to just incorporate. Taste and adjust the seasoning, adding more pepper, salt or balsamic as desired.

SERVING IDEAS: Spread on rustic bread with shaved Parmesan, in a baguette sandwich with prosciutto and arugula, on a toasted poppy-seed bagel or on a buttermilk biscuit with Black Forest ham.

TO STORE: Divide each batch between 2 sheets of parchment paper. Shape and roll each into a cylinder, about 6 inches (15 centimeters) long. Twist the parchment paper at the ends to seal. Refrigerate the butter for at least 2 hours and up to 3 days before serving, or wrap in plastic wrap to freeze for up to 1 month.

Essentials

THE TICKLE-ME-ELMO

Shuddering shoulders, tittering tee-hees, fluttering eyelashes. Be warned:
While this giggle may appear dainty, it's arguably the most contagious.

THE STIFLE

When you know you shouldn't be laughing, this is the closest you can come to preserving your honor.
If not successfully executed, it can give way to its less subtle cousins, the Snort and the Wheezer.

THE EVIL GENIUS

Often heard while tying a distressed damsel to train tracks or filling a mobster's
shoes with cement, this snigger of a laugh has a *hyuk-hyuk-hyuk* intonation.

THE "I CAN'T BELIEVE YOU JUST SAID THAT"

Commonly witnessed near politically incorrect uncles at family gatherings, this laugh
often requires some form of face shielding in a feeble attempt to hide your mirth.

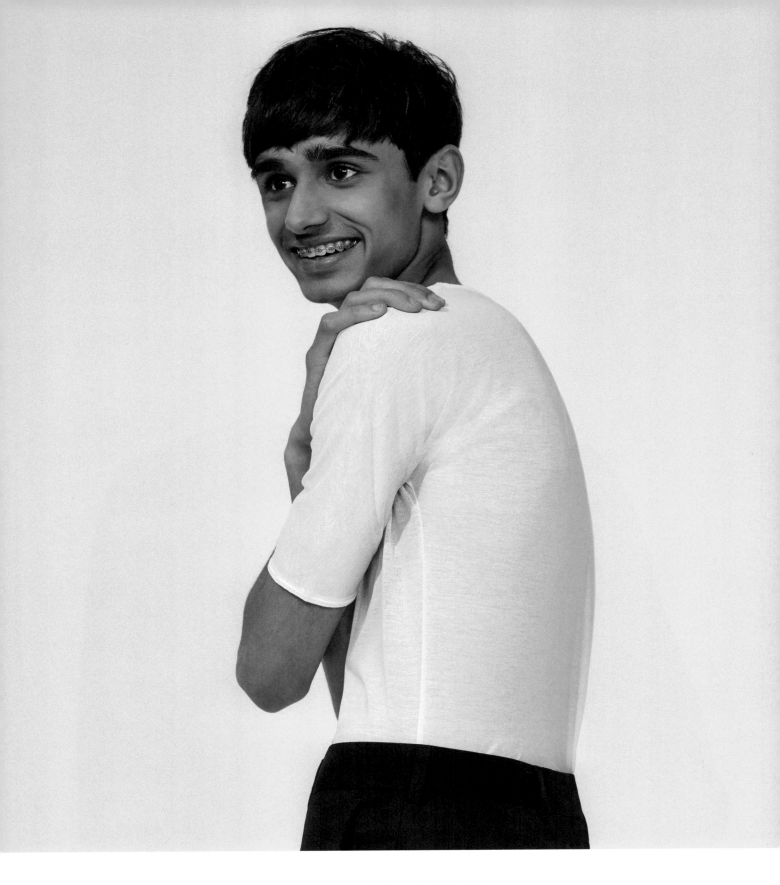

THE UNEXPECTED COMPLIMENT

While you may try to be humble and appreciative when a surprise piece of praise comes your way,
resorting to nervous chuckling and hair twirling is the most common reaction to flattery.

THE INDIGESTION

Tummy-clutching is a sure indication of this often agonizing holler. Other symptoms include
strained facial expressions and being doubled over by a sharp, side-splitting pain in the stomach.

THE LOLCAT

Sometimes the cuteness of the world is just too much for one internet connection to handle.
Sneezing pandas, napping babies and puppies playing in ball pits may also produce this glee.

THE ONOMATOPOEIA

Some roars like these are aptly named after the sounds they mirror. Examples include
the Crow ("*caw-caw-caw*"), the Saint Nick ("*ho-ho-ho*") and the Memory Loss ("*who-who-who*").

WORDS
PETER BLOCK

PHOTOGRAPHS
NICOLE FRANZEN

A SENSE OF BELONGING

The most basic human needs for a happy and healthy life are food, water and shelter, but there's another essential building block required for a well-rounded society: belonging. In Peter Block's book Community: The Structure of Belonging (Berrett-Koehler Publishers, 2009), he explores how we can become better connected citizens on a local level. Here, he introduces the concept, followed by a series of excerpts from his book.

There was a time when belonging and association were built into our culture. The French historian Alexis de Tocqueville traveled to America in 1823 and had one overriding impression: Unlike Europe, Americans are a people drawn to volunteerism and associational life.

Times have changed.

After World War II, much of the Western world climbed the ladder and lost touch with each other. We romanticized mobility, built the highway system and raced to the suburbs. We went in search of home ownership and wanted to live among like-minded people. We chose individuality over belonging, idealized the middle-class career, sacrificed the extended family and adopted a certain "standard of living"—code phrase for consumption—as our goal in life.

This definition of the "good life" has been the domestic narrative for some 200 years. We've become a full consumer society, but if you look closely at your own experience and the larger world, you can see how this belief in growth, expansion, mobility and technology has reached its limits. Relationally, despite the fact that we can text and use Instagram 24/7, we're more isolated. Economically, we've lost our sense of security and a knowable future.

Fortunately, there's a counter-narrative emerging. Our spirit is being renewed. We're moving closer to one another. Small is replacing scale, slow is replacing fast, few are replacing many. There's an alternative economy emerging, and it includes micro-financing, cooperative enterprise, 50-mile food hubs and living within reach and walking distance.

The attraction to this counter-narrative isn't just about lifestyle. It isn't about the land and the air and the water. It's an awakening of our early cultural instincts to care for the common good, to acknowledge that we belong to each other. That we need each other to fulfill what we really care about. As the seductions of the American Dream evaporate, we're realizing that to raise a child to be healthy and to be safe, we have to inhabit a geographical place with people who provide something constant.

To experience a sense of belonging, we need to reclaim our humanity and place more value on the power of relationships. We need to be with people and in situations where our fallibility is accepted rather than treated as something to be fixed. We need to reclaim time, to have time on our hands, time to waste, time for unplanned conversation, time for biding our time. These qualities of belonging are always available to us. Awakening our sense of belonging isn't about remembering the past; it's a re-membering, as in putting our limbs and ourselves back together.

> "To belong is to act as an investor, owner and creator of this place. To be welcome, even if we are strangers."

Community is about the experience of belonging. We're in community each time we find a place where we belong. The word belong has two meanings. First and foremost, to belong is to be related to and a part of something. It's membership, the experience of being at home in the broadest sense of the phrase. It's the opposite of thinking that "wherever I am, I'd be better off somewhere else." Or "I'm still forever wandering, looking for that place where I belong." The opposite of belonging is to feel isolated and always (all ways) on the margin, an outsider. To belong is to know, even in the middle of the night, that I'm among friends.

The second meaning of the word belong has to do with being an owner: Something belongs to me. To belong to a community is to act as a creator and co-owner of that community. What I consider mine I will build and nurture. The work is to seek a wider and deeper sense of emotional ownership in our communities; it means fostering a sense of ownership and accountability among all of a community's citizens.

Belonging can also be thought of as a longing to be. Being is our capacity to find our deeper purpose in all that we do. It's the capacity to be present and to discover our authenticity and whole selves. This is often thought of as an individual capacity, but it's also a community capacity. Community is the container within which our longing to be is fulfilled.

The need to create a structure of belonging grows out of the isolated nature of our lives, our institutions and our communities. The absence of belonging is so widespread that we might say we're living in an age of isolation, imitating the lament from early in the previous century, when life was referred to as the age of anxiety. Ironically, today we talk about how small our world has become, with the shrinking effect of globalization, instant sharing of information, quick technology, workplaces that operate around the globe. Yet these don't necessarily create a sense of belonging. They provide connection, diverse information, an infinite range of opinion. But all this doesn't create the connection from which we can become grounded and experience the sense of safety that arises from a place where we're emotionally, spiritually and psychologically a member.

Our isolation occurs because Western culture, our individualistic narrative, the inward attention of our institutions and our professions and the messages from our media all fragment us. We're broken into pieces.

One aspect of our fragmentation is the gaps between sectors of our cities and neighborhoods; businesses, schools, social service organizations, churches and government operate mostly in their own worlds. Each piece is working hard on its own purpose, but parallel effort added together doesn't make a community. Our communities are separated into silos; they're a collection of institutions and programs operating near one another but not overlapping or touching. This is important to understand because it's this dividedness that makes it so difficult to create a more positive or alternative future—especially in a culture that's much more interested in individuality and independence than in interdependence. The work is to overcome this fragmentation.

To create the sense that we're safe and among friends, especially those we've not yet met, is a particular challenge for our cities and rural towns. The dominant narrative about our cities is that they're unsafe and troubled. Those we label "homeless" or "ex-offenders" or "disabled" or "at risk" are the most visible people who struggle with belonging, but isolation and apartness is also a wider condition of modern life. This is as true in our gated communities and suburbs as in our urban centers.

The cost of our detachment and disconnection isn't only our isolation, our loneliness, but also the fact that there are too many people in our communities whose gifts remain on the margin. Filling the need for belonging isn't just a personal struggle for connection, but also a community problem. The effects of the fragmentation of our communities show up in low voter turnout, the struggle to sustain volunteerism and the large portion of the population who remain disengaged. The struggle is also the reality for the millions of people around the world who are part of today's diaspora—the growing number of displaced people unable to return to their homeland, living and raising their children in a permanent state of transition.

Community offers the promise of belonging and calls for us to acknowledge our interdependence. To belong is to act as an investor, owner and creator of this place. To be welcome, even if we are strangers. As if we came to the right place and are affirmed for that choice.

To feel a sense of belonging is important because it will lead us from conversations about safety and comfort to other conversations, such as our relatedness and willingness to provide hospitality and generosity. Hospitality is the welcoming of strangers, and generosity is an offer with no expectation of return. These are two elements that we want to nurture as we work to create, strengthen and restore our communities. This will not occur in a culture dominated by isolation, and its correlate, fear.

One key perspective is that, to create a more positive and connected future for our communities, we must be willing to trade their problems for their possibilities. This trade is what's necessary to create a future for our cities and neighborhoods, organizations and institutions—a future that's distinct from the past.

To create an alternative future, we need to advance our understanding of the nature of communal or collective transformation. We know a good deal about individual transformation, but our understanding about the transformation of human systems, such as our workplaces, neighborhoods and towns, is primitive at best and too often naive in the belief that, if enough individuals awaken and become intentional and compassionate beings, the shift in community will follow.

The kind of future we're primarily interested in is the way in which communities—whether in the workplace or neighborhood, rural town or urban center—create a wider sense of belonging among their citizens.

This is why we shouldn't be focused on individual transformation. Individual transformation is the more popular conversation, and the choice to not focus on it is because we've already learned that the transformation of large numbers of individuals doesn't result in the transformation of communities. If we continue to invest in individuals as the primary target of change, we'll spend our primary energy on this and never fully invest in communities. In this way, individual transformation comes at the cost of community.

A shift in community benefits from shifts in individual consciousness but needs a communal connectedness as well, a communal structure of belonging that produces the foundation for the whole system to move. This is why it's so frustrating to create high performance and consciousness in individuals, and in individual institutions, and then find that they have so little impact on the social capital or fabric of the community.

Collective change occurs when individuals and small diverse groups engage one another in the presence of many others doing the same. It comes from the knowledge that what's occurring in one space is similarly happening in other spaces, especially ones where I don't know what they're doing. This is the value of a network, or even a network of networks, which is today's version of a social movement.

To stay with this thinking—that communal transformation is about the structure of gathering, letting the right questions evolve and going slow with fewer numbers of people than we'd like—we have to continue to shed certain conventional notions. For example, the dominant belief is that better or more leadership, programs, funding, expertise, studies, training and master plans are the ways to build community. Unfortunately, trying harder at these things gives us just a little more of what we already have. They're the path to improvement but not transformation. Better leadership, funding, training and the like are about fixing a set of symptoms or problems, which is the conventional conversation. What we want

"If we saw others as another aspect of ourselves, we'd welcome them into our midst."

"To belong is to know, even in the middle of the night, that I'm among friends."

to explore is that way of thinking and being in community that allows our goodwill to make a real difference. These are ways of thinking and being that can help us choose a new context and find more effective ways to improve our structure of belonging.

The future is created one room at a time, one gathering at a time. Each gathering needs to become an example of the future we want to create. This means the small group is where transformation takes place. Large-scale transformation occurs when enough small group shifts lead to the larger change. Small groups have the most leverage when they meet as part of a larger gathering. At these moments, citizens experience the intimacy of the small circle and are simultaneously aware that they're part of a larger whole that shares their concerns.

The small group gains power with certain kinds of conversations. To build community, we seek conversations where people show up by invitation rather than mandate and experience an intimate and authentic relatedness. We have conversations where the focus is on the communal possibility and there's a shift in ownership of this place, even though others are in charge. We structure these conversations so that diversity of thinking and dissent are given space, commitments are made without barter and the gifts of each person and our community are acknowledged and valued.

Communal transformation is best initiated through those times when we gather. It's when groups of people are in a room together that a shift in context is noticed, felt and reinforced. This means that each gathering takes on a special importance as a leading indicator of the future. Every meeting or special event is that place where context can be shifted, relatedness can be built and new conversation can be introduced. The times that we gather are when we draw conclusions about what kind of community we live in.

The small group is the structure that allows every voice to be heard. It's in groups of 3 to 12 that intimacy is created. This intimate conversation makes the process personal. It provides the structure where

people overcome isolation and where the experience of belonging is created. Even though we may be in a room filled with a large number of people we'll never meet, by having made intimate contact with a couple of people in our small work group we're brought into connection with all others. The small group is the bridge between our own individual existence and the larger community. In the small group discussion, we discover that our own concerns are more universal than we imagined. This discovery that we're not alone—that others can at least understand what's on our mind, if not agree with us—is what created the feeling of belonging. When this occurs in the same place and time, in the presence of a larger community, the collective possibility begins to take form and have legs.

The power of the small group cannot be overemphasized. Something almost mystical, certainly mysterious occurs when citizens sit in a small group, for they often become more authentic and personal with each other there than in other settings. Designing small group conversations is so simple that it rarely receives the attention and importance it deserves.

After we finish giving speeches about the virtues of our neighborhood and city, we love to elaborate their problems. For years we've studied and reported the problems of housing, health care, the environment, youth at risk, race, the disabled, poverty, unemployment, public education, the crisis in transportation and drugs. These problems are studied by academics and fueled by talk radio and the AM band, which serves as a place for hosts and citizens to argue, debate and complain about who's right or wrong and who needs to change. Talk radio and TV are the visible barometers of our attachment to the context giving primacy to problems.

Our love of problems runs deeper than just the joy of complaint, being right or escape from responsibility. The core belief from which we operate is that an alternative or better future can be accomplished by more problem solving. We believe that defining, analyzing and studying problems is the way to make a better world. It's the dominant mind-set of Western culture.

This context—that life is a set of problems to be solved—may actually limit any chance of the future being different from the past. The interest we have in problems is so intense that at some point we take our identity from those problems. Without them, it seems like we wouldn't know who we are as a community. Many of the strongest advocates for change would lose their sense of identity if the change they desired ever occurred.

To shift to some other context, we need to detach ourselves from the discussions of problems. One payoff for believing that problems and the suffering in our cities are the inevitable products of modern life and culture is that it lets us off the hook. The payoff begins the moment we believe that problems reside in others and that they're the ones who need to change. We displace or assign to others certain qualities that have more to do with us than with them. This is called projection, an idea most of us are quite familiar with. I discuss it here because if we don't take back our projections, a new context and conversation are simply not possible. The essence of our projection is that it places accountability for an alternative future on others. This is the payoff of stereotyping, prejudice and a bunch of "isms" that we're all familiar with. This is what produces the "other." The reward is that it takes the pressure off of us. It's a welcome escape from our freedom. We project onto leaders the qualities or disappointments that we find too much to carry ourselves. We project onto the stranger, the wounded, the enemy those aspects of ourselves that are too much to own.

Projection denies the fact that my view of the "other" is my creation, and this is especially true with how we view our communities and the people in them. Most simply, how I view the other is an extension or template of how I view myself. This insight is the essence of being accountable. To be accountable is to act as an owner and creator of what exists in the world, including the light and dark corners of my own

existence. It's the willingness to focus on what we can do in the face of whatever the world presents to us. Accountability doesn't project or deny; accountability is the willingness to see the whole picture that resides within, even what's not so pretty.

The projection is the attribution we make, the conclusions we draw and the fact that all we see in them is what's missing. When we believe that the "other" is the problem and that transformation is required of them and not of us, we become the beneficiaries of their suffering in the world. Some of us make a living off of their deficiencies. We study their needs, devise professions to service them, create institutions dependent on the existence of these deficiencies. All done with sincere intent and in the name of virtue.

To continue as a community to focus on the needs and deficiencies of the most vulnerable isn't an act of hospitality. It substitutes labeling for welcoming. It's isolating in that they become a special category of people, defined by what they cannot do. This isolates the most vulnerable. Despite our care for them, we don't welcome them into our midst, we service them. They become objects. This may be why it's easier to raise money for suffering in distant places or to celebrate the history of slavery's end than it is to raise money for our neighbors on the margin who are six blocks away. Their proximity stands in the way of our compassion.

In our philanthropy, this mind-set that the "other" is the problem means that we need to wait for them to change before the change we want in the world can come to pass. And until they change, we need to stay distant and contain them. This diverts us from the realization that we have the means, the tools, the thinking to create a world we want to inhabit, and to do it for all. If we saw others as another aspect of ourselves, we'd welcome them into our midst. We'd let them know that they belong, that they're neighbors, with all their complexity.

Restorative community is created when we allow ourselves to use the language of healing and relatedness and belonging

"We need to be with people and in situations where our fallibility is accepted rather than treated as something to be fixed."

without embarrassment. It recognizes that taking responsibility for one's own part in creating the present situation is the critical act of courage and engagement, which is the axis around which the future rotates. The essence of restorative community building isn't economic prosperity or the political discourse or the capacity of leadership; it's citizens' willingness to own up to their contribution, to be humble, to choose accountability and to have faith in their own capacity to make authentic promises to create the alternative future.

This means that the essential aspect of the restoration of community is a context in which each citizen chooses to be accountable rather than entitled.

Accountability is the willingness to care for the whole, and it flows out of the kind of conversations we have about the new story we want to take our identity from. It means we have conversations of what we can do to create the future. Entitlement is a conversation about what others can or need to do to create the future for us.

Restoration begins when we think of community as a possibility, a declaration of the future that we choose to live in. This idea of a communal possibility is distinct from what we commonly call an individual possibility. Community is something more than a collection of individual longings, desires or possibilities.

The communal possibility has its own landscape, and its own dynamics, requirements and points of leverage. In the individualistic world we live in, we can congregate a large collection of self-actualized people and still not hold the idea or experience of community. The communal possibility rotates on the question "What can we create together?" This emerges from the social space we create when we're together. It's shaped by the nature of the culture within which we operate but isn't controlled by it. This question of what we can create together is at the intersection of possibility and accountability. Possibility without accountability results in a wishful thinking. Accountability without possibility creates despair, for even if we know we're creating the world we exist

in, we cannot imagine it being any different from the past that got us here.

The future of a community then becomes a choice between a retributive conversation (a problem to be solved) and a restorative conversation (a possibility to be lived in). Restoration is a possibility brought into being by choosing that kind of conversation. And with that conversation it becomes real and tangible, for once we've declared a possibility, and done so with a sense of belonging and in the presence of others, that possibility has been brought into the room, and thus into the institution, into the community.

The key phrase here is "in the presence of others." A possibility—when declared publicly, witnessed by others with whom we have a common interest, at a moment when something is at stake—is a critical element of communal transformation. This public conversation creates a larger relatedness and transcends a simply individual transformation. Conversations of possibility gone public aren't all that restores, but without them personal and private conversations of possibility have no political currency and therefore no communal power.

What these have in common is the movement from centrism and individualism to pluralism and interdependent communalism. This shift has important consequences for our communities. It offers to return politics to public service and restore our trust in leadership. It moves us from having faith in professionals and those in positions of authority to having faith in our neighbors. It takes us into a context of hospitality, wherein we welcome strangers rather than believing we need to protect ourselves from them. It changes our mindset from valuing what's efficient to valuing the importance of belonging. It helps us to leave behind our penchant for seeing our disconnectedness as an inevitable consequence of modern life and moves us toward accountability and citizenship.

"We need to reclaim time, to have time on our hands, time to waste, time for unplanned conversation, time for biding our time."

INTERVIEW
RACHEL EVA LIM

PHOTOGRAPHS
ANDERS SCHØNNEMANN

STYLING
NATHALIE SCHWER

A Day in the Life: Stine Gam & Enrico Fratesi

Since launching a furniture design studio in 2006, Stine Gam and Enrico Fratesi have split their time between her native Copenhagen and his hometown of Pesaro in Italy. Although their growing business, GamFratesi, requires a wayfaring lifestyle, they've found ways to keep themselves grounded thanks to the daily rituals they engage in while traveling and the time they set aside for family.

Stine Gam and Enrico Fratesi have managed to achieve a lifestyle many of us only dream about: The founders and designers behind the furniture studio GamFratesi travel regularly between their hometowns of Pesaro, Italy, and Copenhagen, Denmark. While the couple often misses the comforting rhythms of daily home life with their three-year-old son, Frederik, traveling has been a fertile ground for creative inspiration. Their designs, though rooted in the stark and practical Scandinavian tradition, incorporate conceptual elements that add a touch of playfulness to their minimalist aesthetic. Running a young company keeps Stine and Enrico busy, but they still make it a priority to carve out time for friends, family and lingering over scrumptious breakfasts each morning. We spoke with the pair about how their family stays in the present while hopping between homes.

What kind of families did you grow up in? Were there any life lessons your parents passed down to you? — *Stine*: We grew up in two very different environments. We recently found an old black-and-white photograph of Enrico's father at the age of six, sitting in a workshop while his father made shoes for postwar survivors. We inherited a sense of discipline and a pure dedication to our work from him, as well as the knowledge that everything is possible if you're committed and put in the work. We also found a photograph of my 30-year-old father from when he had long hair and was climbing a tree with his guitar. We got the freedom to dream and express ourselves without boundaries from him. These are two very different lessons, though both are equally important to us.

What are some of the differences between the Italian and Danish approaches to life? — *Enrico*: The Danes are true masters of creating intimate and welcoming domestic spaces. Perhaps this is due to the adverse Scandinavian weather conditions that force them to stay indoors all the time and encourage them to create warm and inviting home environments. They have a knack for adapting their homes to accommodate natural light, have a great eye for color and know how to bring aspects of nature into their everyday lives. In Italy, people seem to gravitate more toward gathering in communal areas such as large city squares rather than staying inside. More attention is paid to quality and developing these spaces rather than focusing on interiors. That said, we sometimes come across interesting historical interiors that mix unexpected styles and objects with sophisticated design solutions.

How do the work ethics in Denmark and Italy differ? — *Stine*: When we're in Copenhagen, we allow ourselves to linger over breakfast in the kitchen, making conversation and enjoying the food and each other's company. This is less common in Italy, where morning meals usually consist of a quick espresso and a croissant at the bar. The Italians prioritize lunch instead and tend to spend a long time partaking in this meal.

Please tell us a bit about your weekday morning routines at home: Do you have any personal rituals? — *Enrico*: I'm quite grumpy in the morning while Stine is calm and very good at gathering the family around the table for a wonderful, cozy breakfast. Our days often begin with homemade bread and cookies, fresh juice and chatting and playing with our son, Frederik, before we start our day. Stine loves mornings as she feels like she has the entire day in front her. I'm more partial to evenings as they feel like the calm after the storm of the day's activities.

How do you like to spend time when you're at home? — *Stine*: Listening to music, preparing some nice food in the kitchen, reading books and playing with our son. Our home is located above a busy street and we enjoy people-watching from our window. We also like going on long walks around Copenhagen if the weather outside is nice.

What are your after-work hobbies? — *Stine*: We're lucky that our work is also our passion and that our hobbies are all somewhat art- or design-related. Many of them become inspiration for our work, such as reading or listening to good music. We love these art forms for their expressive abilities and how they're able to convey a wealth of emotions in just a few words or notes.

How do you like to spend your weekends? — *Enrico*: Apart from certain situations where an imminent delivery forces us to work, we devote our weekends to the family, experiencing the city and meeting friends. We've hoped for and have been working toward having nonworking weekends for so many years, but we've only recently achieved this goal.

How often do you host dinner parties? — *Enrico*: We love having our friends over to our house for fortnightly meals. We often serve a simple, family-style meal made using a small selection of high quality seasonal ingredients. Lunch is often Danish-style and consists of bread and an assortment of Scandinavian root vegetables. For dinner, we like serving well-made Italian pasta with a slow-roasted tomato sauce.

What are the most important components to running a business? — *Enrico*: Passion and patience.

What do you enjoy most about traveling? — *Stine*: Traveling has always been an integral part of our working process. We used to have more freedom and flexibility in the early stages of our company, but growing business opportunities in Copenhagen have required us to establish it as our primary work base and Pesaro as a refuge for when we need some time away from the city. We allow ourselves to make the trip to Pesaro when things get too hectic. It's a lovely city nestled between the sea and the hills. Everything is within walking distance and the rustic buildings provide a welcome contrast to the highly stylized and modern architecture you find in Copenhagen. It's essential for us to maintain a strong relationship with each location, and each has a special place in our hearts.

Are there any simple traditions you try to preserve when you're traveling around in different cities? — *Stine*: A key part of our everyday routine is valuing the little things and individual moments in the day. We try to implement this philosophy regardless of where we are in the world.

What do you miss most about home when you're traveling? — *Enrico*: We miss our son like crazy when he's not with us. We don't long for any material things when we're away, though we do miss the everyday routines that come with being in your own home, such as walking around barefoot in the kitchen or preparing a bowl of yogurt and muesli and enjoying it on the couch while chatting for hours. The first thing we do after returning from a long trip is to whip up something to eat, often a dish that's simple and homey.

How do you strike a balance between the time you spend at work and the time you spend with friends and family? — *Enrico*: While the fact that we're self-employed means that we invest tons of passion, dedication and time into our work, family comes first. We've had to make many personal sacrifices over the years for the sake of our business, but we make it a point not to let work compromise family time.

How do you manage to stay true to the traditional aspects of European design while experimenting with new methods and techniques? — *Enrico*: We don't think that you can create something out of nothing. Likewise, designers ought to have a thorough knowledge of what's come before. Our present gestures are dictated by our past, and we believe that true innovation comes from taking traditional design practices and developing them in new and exciting ways.

What are some of your favorite aspects of Italian and Danish design? How are they different? — *Stine*: Coming from two different cultures has been instrumental in how we've approached our design process. We strive to bring a sense of diversity to our designs. We have a deep respect for the Scandinavian masters of the past, as their work utilized craftsmanship and quality materials to create functional and honest designs. We also admire the Italian masters for their intellectual approach to design. From this cross-cultural substrate, we create furniture that respectfully reflects both traditions while also featuring unique embedded stories, symbols and associations, often expressed in a minimalist aesthetic.

In what ways has your work as a designer influenced your interior decorating process? — *Stine*: As designers, we're pretty analytical and critical when it comes to interior decorating. We believe in quality over quantity and we'd rather have a sparse home than one filled with meaningless items that only add to the clutter. We have a variety of classical pieces in our home, though we like changing things up every once in a while by rearranging the furniture or seeing how the new pieces fit in with the overall vibe of the home.

What's your philosophy on material possessions in the home? How do you determine which things are essential or will add value to your home life? — *Enrico*: I love collecting small objects and believe that there's nothing more beautiful than beautiful things! But beautiful objects don't necessarily have to be expensive or luxurious. Beauty comes in many shades, and it's often surprising, unusual or unexpected choices that make an item interesting and give it a sense of beauty. Stine is less preoccupied with material things and finds it easy to live with less.

Is there a philosophy behind your company, GamFratesi? What kind of impact does it have on your daily design process? — *Enrico*: Our design process takes its creative drive from a fusion of tradition and renewal. We aim to create furniture that illustrates the process and the techniques that created it, which reflects a persistent exploration of the diverse border zone between harmony and disharmony. We believe that it's somewhere in between these qualities that you can obtain a sense of reflection and clarity.

Why do simplicity, function and minimalism appeal to you? — *Stine*: Simplicity, function and minimalism are words that encompass the meaning of honesty. As designers, we believe that honesty should be the foundation of our work.

What do you consider the most important elements when it comes to creating a great design? — *Stine*: Try approaching the process organically. Don't set out with the end goal being creating a great design. Think, create and question your products and be willing to fail and start all over again at any time in the process. While our work originates from a personal place, we come up with our designs based on the needs of the customer. Society and the way that people approach furniture and design are constantly evolving, and we strive to meet the changing needs of our community with each project we undertake.

ILLUSTRATIONS
CHRISTOPHE LOUIS

Words with Friends

Whether you're a quiet person or a loud talker, your conversational skills can enhance your social interactions. Breaking down the act of communication into its core components—tone, listening, language and silence—allows us to engage with more thought, understanding and consideration.

WORDS
RACHEL EVA LIM

TONE

When it comes to conversation, it's not just what we say but how we say it that matters. Our intonation can often be more reflective of our true intentions than the words we utter.

Imagine a world where human beings spoke exclusively in robotic, monotonous drones. Where subtly, irony and sarcasm no longer existed and deadpan was not a style of comedic delivery but a way of life. Where misinterpretation was a standard component of everyday conversation that was no longer reserved for the digital realm. Where heartfelt declarations of affection or streams of expletives directed at the TV were dispensed in the same unfeeling pitch as an order at the neighborhood juice bar.

If language provides the raw ingredients for good conversation, tone denotes the way that these components are prepped, seasoned, garnished and ultimately delivered onto the plates of waiting diners with a graceful flourish. The inflections inherent in our speech patterns are the vocal equivalent of body language—non-linguistic indicators that work to enhance the meaning and emotions already present in the words themselves. Far from playing second fiddle to semantics, these vocal modulations and intonations deeply affect the ways we express our feelings, communicate information and approach our interactions with others.

Subtle discrepancies between our tone and words have a knack for revealing how we truly feel about a situation, whether we want them to or not. While a nervous trill serves to exacerbate the awkwardness of small talk, laughter delivered in a halting and lackluster cadence is probably a good indication that your grand punch line has sadly fallen flat. But this phenomenon can also be used to our advantage if we're conscious of it, allowing us to catch unsuspecting culprits in a lie or confidently storm our way through a presentation at work despite having an iffy grasp of the jargon we're spouting. It can also aid us in inferring that a friend is having a rough time despite her repeated insistence that she's doing "just fine," giving us the green light to dash over to her place with a bottle of the hard stuff and a much-needed shoulder.

The author Samuel Butler once wrote, "We are not won by arguments that we can analyze, but by tone and temper, by the manner which is the man himself." Our voices are natural extensions of our personalities and attitudes: When harnessed in the right way, they inject our language with an added element of conviction, expose shades and degrees of our underlying selves and add significant emotional layers to our daily exchanges.

Living in the digital age means that conversations are often filtered through multiple social networking sites and can reflect the cold glare of our computer screens. While such widespread modes of communication get two emoji thumbs-up for convenience, the expressive and nuanced nature of an in-person exchange offers a sense of honesty that we can't glean from the virtual world. Yes, our tone's uncanny ability to divulge our true emotions can render face-to-face communication messy, vulnerable and downright scary, but that's also what makes it all the more intimate, exhilarating and wonderfully human.

WORDS
ANNU SUBRAMANIAN

LISTENING

Instead of politely nodding while you wait for your chance to speak, try truly listening. It takes more deliberate concentration than simply keeping your lips sealed.

We all have *those* friends: the ones who regale us with stories of distant travel, passionate love affairs and celebrity run-ins. The ones who command our attention with their sparkling anecdotes and wry wit. The ones who thrill, enthrall, dazzle. Yet those aren't the ones who burn brightest in our memory. The friends we value most are the curious ones, the ones who ask and remember: the listeners.

Unfortunately, the word *listening* evokes the image of leaning across a table, hands clasped in ostentatious earnest. Their eyebrows furrow like an accordion exhaling, and their lips purse sympathetically. Their nodding and reassuring cooing makes us feel more babysat than listened to—or pitied or smothered. On the other hand, how exhilarating is it to talk to a friend who honestly listens? To have a relationship filled with genuine wide-eyed glee or the unthinking instinct to clasp another's hand at just the right moment?

There may not be a guidebook to listening, but being present is paramount. Listening shouldn't be defined in terms of passivity or silence: Giving someone your attention is active and empowering. Skilled listeners wrench themselves away from the passel of thoughts and questions that thunder through the brain and, like an arrow pointing to a spot on a map, convey that they are here.

Perhaps the greatest affront to true listening is our own need to contribute. Rather than allow someone to reach the full extent of her own insights, even if that takes a few false starts or thoughtful silences, our impulse can be to gather our own thoughts and then seamlessly lob back a talking point. While we might deny ourselves the urge to interject, we're furiously searching through our own mental filing cabinets, digging for an apt mirroring anecdote, word of advice or charming wisecrack. We sit still as a friend finishes her story, but our response is already cued up and ready to deliver, despite what that ending might be. In those moments, receiving someone's pointed advice or a "that happened to me too!" can diminish a relationship more than create closeness. It dilutes. It turns an individual experience into a drop in a stream of similar ones.

This sort of behavior can be as rude as blatantly interrupting. After all, we make a choice to share, so when we do it's often because we just want someone to hear us. This gets to the heart of why listening is so much more essential to a relationship than sharing similar interests or having the ability to charm: Listening helps us feel understood, and the best listeners make us feel necessary.

Listening takes practice, but once you've mastered it, thinking and effort fall away and are replaced by the totality of sharing a life-bracing moment. That's why listening doesn't mean a conversation is half-silent. Instead, it has verve. Neither party feels diminished for talking—and we respond more thoughtfully in return.

WORDS
AMY WOODROFFE

LANGUAGE

Most of us are capable of forming coherent sentences, but a carefully considered vocabulary and a better understanding of how to use it can help us become better communicators.

The average person is likely to say 370 million words in a lifetime. What a mysterious blessing it is to explore ourselves with such a vocabulary, voice our emotional highs and lows, share ideas and discuss all the possible pizza topping combinations. But we don't often choose our words wisely, and we certainly don't often appreciate what a wonder it is they're there to mangle in the first place.

Most healthy humans are born with the innate urge to coo, then babble, then talk. As soon as we're able to make sounds, we start listening to the other ones around us, smooshing syllables together and slotting words into the awaiting Rolodex of our minds. By age four, words are so accessible that we barely have to think in order to express them, but our subconscious command of speech can easily become a curse as we grow older and more careless. In moments of linguistic weakness, we can fall prey to verbal landslides where we incessantly babble a mess of words we'll have to clean up later. When we forget to think before we speak, our words can betray our true meanings—or reveal them.

The benefits of a carefully constructed sentence have been pondered by the philosophical greats for millennia. Greek philosophers encouraged us to nurture our evolutionary gift for the gab, emphasizing the importance of a sizable vocabulary and the cultural context in which to place it. And that means reading. In his books on rhetoric, Aristotle urged that we must learn philosophy and psychology before we can truly speak well. Building our mental library of words allows us to wax lyrical on more subjects and with more panache, and it also adds a layer of nuance to what would otherwise be an adjectiveless sentence.

But developing a true understanding of language is more complicated than simply turning your brain into a dictionary. Having a conversation about, let's say, pizza, requires a number of things to happen: First, the Broca's area of the brain organizes a set of conventional sound units. Next, our highly evolved musculature conducts and the larynx, tongue, jaw and lips generate a series of sounds with symphony-like control. The listener's brain decodes and interprets the odd sounds, and within a matter of seconds we're debating the necessity of cheese crusts.

Words are our most powerful tool for self-expression and relationship building, but they also directly inform our own thoughts. Consider how you're thinking right now—would you be feeling this way or contemplating this article's premise accurately if it wasn't for the words whizzing through your brain? Expanding our vocabularies and getting a tighter grip on our own handle of language doesn't just make us better communicators: It also helps us to be better, more self-aware people.

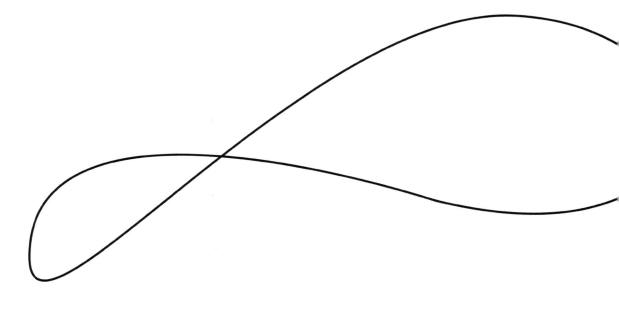

WORDS
ANNE FULLERTON

SILENCE

Search the self-help section and you'll find an abundance of advice on how to keep a conversation flowing. However, when we rush to fill in the gaps, we often miss something profound.

We've all been there: embarrassed and shifting in our chairs, keenly aware of our surroundings, our eyes roaming desperately around the room for something, anything, that we can grasp to keep from sliding further into the chasm of awkward silence. The longer the hush persists, the harder it becomes to clamber out. The stakes on what we say next seem to double with every passing second. Our bodies often respond to a break in conversation the same way they would to a fast-approaching predator, which seems particularly cruel. After all, neither flight nor fight is an option when you're in your favorite mid-priced Italian restaurant staring at a new acquaintance across the table. Instead, we must sit passively as our ego is torn apart and devoured like the evening's antipasti.

The Western world seems to fear silence above all other conversational perils, so nothing fills us with panic quite like an unanticipated break in a dinner-table debate. Some have blamed this on the influence of the ancient Greeks, who revered oration, while others put it down to our constant exposure to digital distraction. Either way, it hasn't always been this way. At various points in history, the ability to be silent in the company of others has been viewed as an essential part of being good company rather than as the sign of a dullard.

Instead of beating ourselves up next time small talk fails us, why not remind ourselves of the Roman writer Cicero, who believed that "silence is one of the great arts of conversation"? Or we could take solace in the teachings of Taoist philosophers, who became so disillusioned with politics and war that they considered silence a mark of honesty. We could even call on the writings of 20th-century novelist Anaïs Nin, who imbued shared moments of public stillness with an undercurrent of desire. (This theory would make silent rush hour train commutes all kinds of awkward, but at least it provides great consolation when we run out of banter between the main course and dessert.)

Although they differed wildly in their interpretations, Cicero, the Taoists and Nin were on to something. Silence is important, honest and intimate—and that's precisely why it has the power to make us squirm. When we do finally muster the courage to let the seconds pass uninterrupted, we can share something far more valuable than whatever anecdote that might have come before it. We stop performing as ourselves in order to simply be ourselves, and we allow our company to do the same. Instead of viewing silence as a sign of boredom or disinterest, we could see it for what it is: the ultimate expression of acceptance. Sitting beside another person, lost in private thought, is perhaps the highest compliment we can pay them. To paraphrase the words of *Pulp Fiction*'s Mia Wallace, "That's when you know you've found somebody special—when you can just shut up for a minute and comfortably enjoy the silence."

ESSAY
ALICA FORNERET

PHOTOGRAPHS
ANDERS SCHØNNEMANN

STYLING
KATHRIN KOSCHITZKI & SIDSEL RUDOLPH

Tickled Pink

Whether we slice them into triangles, blend them into slushies or wear them on our heads, watermelons are a quintessential part of summer. On the following pages, we've outlined a menu that puts a whole melon to use in a number of refreshing ways.

The return of long summer hikes and muggy afternoons typically inspires a change in our eating habits. After scarfing heaping piles of holiday ham and starchy casseroles during our hip-rounding hibernation, it's a relief for our stomachs and minds to embrace the season's bounty when the sunshine pushes fresh fruit from the earth and into our hands.

While the best watermelons sound hollow when tapped, there's plenty of substance—in both character and stature—to this gargantuan fruit. Its delicious pink flesh is a great reward after labor-intensive summer activities such as lugging one across the park to find a perfect picnic spot, and it's a juicy recompense for figuring out how to crack through the tough rind when you've forgotten a knife (a coin and a lot of patience will eventually get you there). Watermelons allow us to regress into a playful state of mind where spitting seeds off the side of a bridge provides simple entertainment during summer flings or pit stops on road trips. And unlike a holiday pie binge, gorging on watermelon is indulgent in a way that allows face-stuffing without guilt and hedonistic dripping without stains.

In the American South, the summer months encourage methods of watermelon celebration that are rarely matched with other foods. In addition to traditional melon eating, seed spitting and carving contests, there are activities that draw out our creative impulses, such as designing costumes seen on kids wobbling through fairgrounds with striped green football helmets on their heads. But if you're just looking for ways to eat melons, there are more ways to enjoy them beyond the pleasure derived from a simple slice: They can be grilled, added to cocktails, transformed into salsa and used in salads or dressings, and the rinds can even be salvaged and turned into pickled snacks. Other cultures offer a variety of ideas as well: The streets of Mexico City are lined with vendors who dust long chunks with chili powder, soak them in lime and sprinkle them with salt. In France, the melon baller at the back of the drawer is used to make spheres to drop into glasses of *rosé-pamplemousse*. In Vietnam, the seeds are often saved and roasted for New Year celebrations, and in Turkmenistan, the fruit is often preserved as a jelly for year-round enjoyment with tea.

There are some smart ways to maximize your watermelon-choosing success, because there's no greater disappointment than cracking open the rind to find mealy, bland flesh: If you thump a melon and it sounds hollow, then it's ripe and ready to eat. An ideal specimen should show little contrast between the skin's stripes on the top, and the underside should be cream- or yellow-colored. But if you end up with an unappealing slice despite your best intentions, there is hope: Blend it, freeze it, and let the cubes keep your lemonade cold while porch sitting on a sunny afternoon.

SERVES 4

PINK GIN COCKTAIL
WITH GRILLED WATERMELON

This refreshing cocktail will start off your warm summer evening right with a kick of gin, honey, lime and verbena.

½ medium seedless watermelon
    (about 2 ¼ pounds or 1 kilogram)
4 fluid ounces (120 milliliters) gin
1 tablespoon honey, preferably acacia
3 limes
¼ cup (5 grams) fresh lemon verbena,
    lemon balm or mint leaves, plus
    more for garnish
¼ cup sugar
Ice cubes, for serving

Peel the watermelon and cut half of it into small cubes and the other half into larger wedges. Put the cubes into a blender along with the gin and honey. Add the finely grated zest and juice of the first lime, plus the juice of a second lime. Blend until the mixture is smooth and frothy. Let the cocktail stand for 5 minutes to infuse the flavors.

Pulse the lemon verbena and sugar in a food processor until the herb is very finely minced and blended with the sugar. Transfer the mixture to a small plate and set aside.

Meanwhile, heat a grill pan over high heat until smoking hot. Grill the watermelon wedges until marks appear, 1 to 2 minutes per side. Arrange the grilled melon on a platter and sprinkle with the finely grated zest and the juice of the third lime and a little coarsely chopped lemon verbena.

Rub the rim of 4 cocktail glasses with one of the squeezed limes to lightly moisten, then dip it in the sugar mixture to get an even coating. Fill the glasses with ice and pour in the cocktail through a fine strainer. Serve immediately with the warm grilled watermelon.

SERVES 4

WATERMELON SALAD WITH CILANTRO, GINGER AND CHILI

Adding fresh herbs, ginger and chilies to this juicy fruit creates a delectable balance of spicy sweetness.

½ medium seedless watermelon
    (about 2 ¼ pounds or 1 kilogram)
1 lemon
3 tablespoons extra-virgin olive oil
1 small fresh red chili, such as cherry
    bomb or red jalapeño, seeded
    and minced
1 teaspoon fresh ginger, grated
Salt and freshly ground pepper
1 handful fresh cilantro or mint leaves,
    coarsely chopped

Peel the watermelon, cut into large cubes and put in a large bowl.

Add the finely grated lemon zest and juice, olive oil, chili, ginger, a big pinch of salt and several grinds of pepper. Mix gently to coat the watermelon in the marinade. Set aside for at least 20 minutes to marinate before serving (the salad can be refrigerated for up to 4 hours before serving).

Strain off some of the marinade, taste and adjust the seasoning. Serve the watermelon in a large shallow bowl topped with the cilantro or mint.

SERVES 4

GRILLED TUNA WITH WATERMELON AND TARRAGON VINAIGRETTE

The combination of this summer grilled seafood staple with a warm, fruity vinaigrette will elevate any barbecue.

1 ⅓ pounds (600 grams) fresh ahi tuna,
    cut into 4 fillets
½ cup (120 milliliters) extra-virgin olive oil,
    plus more for drizzling
Salt and freshly ground pepper
½ cup (75 grams) black olives,
    such as kalamata or Gaeta, pitted
2 shallots, thinly sliced
1 lemon
1 tablespoon honey, preferably acacia
1 ½ cups (210 grams) seedless
    watermelon, diced
⅓ cup (5 grams) fresh tarragon leaves

Place the tuna on a platter and drizzle lightly with olive oil, rubbing it in to coat both sides nicely. Sprinkle generously with salt and pepper and set aside for about 20 minutes.

In a medium saucepan, combine the olive oil, olives, shallots, lemon zest and juice, honey, ½ teaspoon of salt and several grinds of pepper. Heat gently over medium-low heat just to warm through. Stir in the watermelon and tarragon and remove the pan from the heat. Taste and adjust the seasoning, then set aside.

Meanwhile, prepare a hot fire in a gas or charcoal grill, or heat a grill pan over high heat until smoking hot. Grill the tuna just until grill marks appear and the inside remains pink, about 1 minute on each side. Be careful not to overcook the tuna—it's best served rare.

Rest the tuna fillets for about 2 minutes before cutting each into several slices. Arrange the slices on individual plates or on a large platter to serve family-style, and spoon the warm vinaigrette on top. Serve with good bread.

MAKES ABOUT 1 QUART / 1 LITER

WATERMELON AND COCONUT MILK ICE CREAM

This pastel-colored frozen dessert is made with just four simple ingredients, leaving you more time to relax.

4 cups (600 grams) seedless
   watermelon, diced
1 can (13.5 ounces/400 milliliters)
   full-fat coconut milk, shaken
¼ cup (60 milliliters) light agave syrup
Juice of 1 large lemon

Blend the watermelon, coconut milk, agave syrup and lemon juice in a blender until completely liquefied.

FREEZING OPTION 1:
Churn the mixture in an ice cream machine, using the manufacturer's instructions. Serve immediately if you like the soft, slushy texture, or transfer it to a container, cover and freeze until firm, at least 4 hours.

FREEZING OPTION 2:
Pour the mixture into a large baking dish, cover with plastic wrap and place it in the freezer until frozen, but not quite solid, about 4 hours. Break up the frozen mixture into pieces and place them in a food processor. Process until the texture is as smooth as your desired consistency. Transfer the ice cream to a container, cover and return it to the freezer until firm, at least 4 hours.

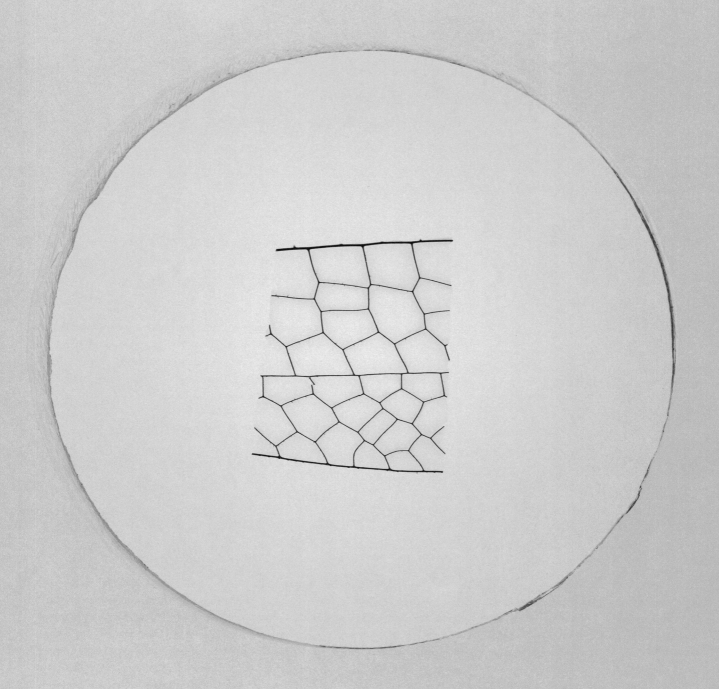

FIG. 01: Dragonfly wing

WORDS
GEORGIA FRANCES KING

PHOTOGRAPHS
JUSTIN FANTL

Under the Microscope

Aristotle may have claimed that the whole is greater than the sum of its parts, but that didn't stop Los Angeles photographer Justin Fantl from spending some time slicing and dicing common objects to see what he could discern from their core components.

Synecdoche is one of those half-remembered words that conjures memories of our high school English classrooms where we first learned to use *juxtaposition* correctly in a sentence. But unlike fancy words that serve to plump our linguistic egos, synecdoche strips stuff down to the foundations of what something really is: a smaller part representing the whole. A set of wheels references the whole car, not just the rounds it rolls on, and a crown can represent not just a king but a whole ruling empire. In the same way, a single seemingly impersonal element can accurately represent a larger intimate construct, just as the sound of a dinner bell recalls memories of our grandmother's cooking, or the smell of Play-Doh can remind us of our childhood. If we turn this literary theory inward, it forces us to determine the smallest parts of our personalities that best represent us as individuals. If we put ourselves under the microscope, what would we see? And how would others perceive us? Perhaps they'd notice that cluster of freckles on our forehead, left over from many summer lake vacations with too much fun and too little sunscreen, or the color of our eyes when it's stormy or the dimple that only appears when we're really, *really* smiling. When we consider what our lives might look like when cross-sectioned and divided, we can form a better understanding of who we are at the foundation rather than our surface projections. If we treated life this way instead of focusing on the big picture, we would pay more attention to the details and less to the paralyzing waves of overwhelming information. By closely studying and observing ourselves and those around us, we may be able to form a better understanding of who we are and the people who matter to us.

FIG. 02: Mouth part of butterfly

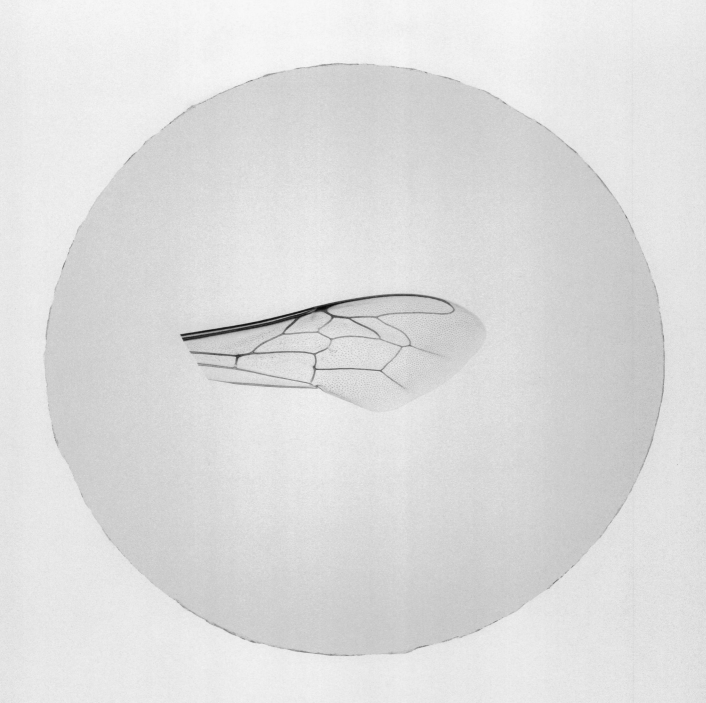

FIG. 03: Bee wing

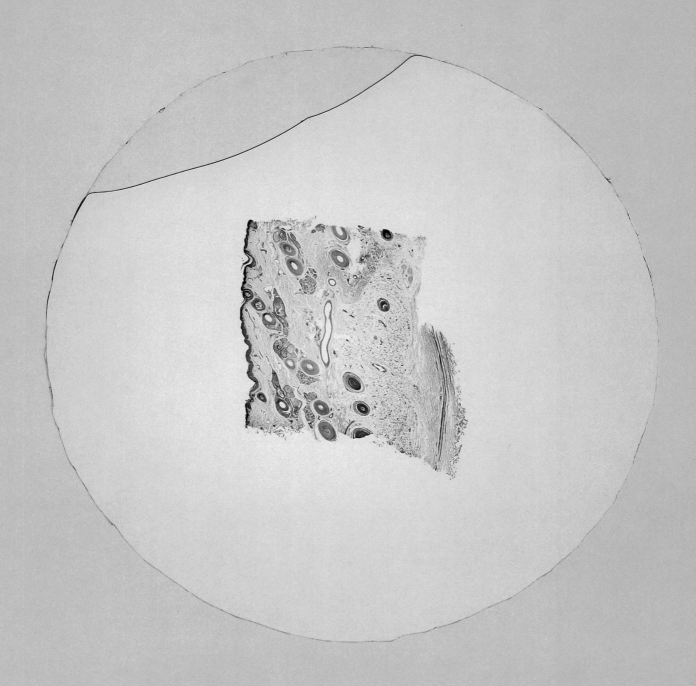

FIG. 04: Human skin with hair follicle

FIG. 05: Pollen-carrying leg of honeybee

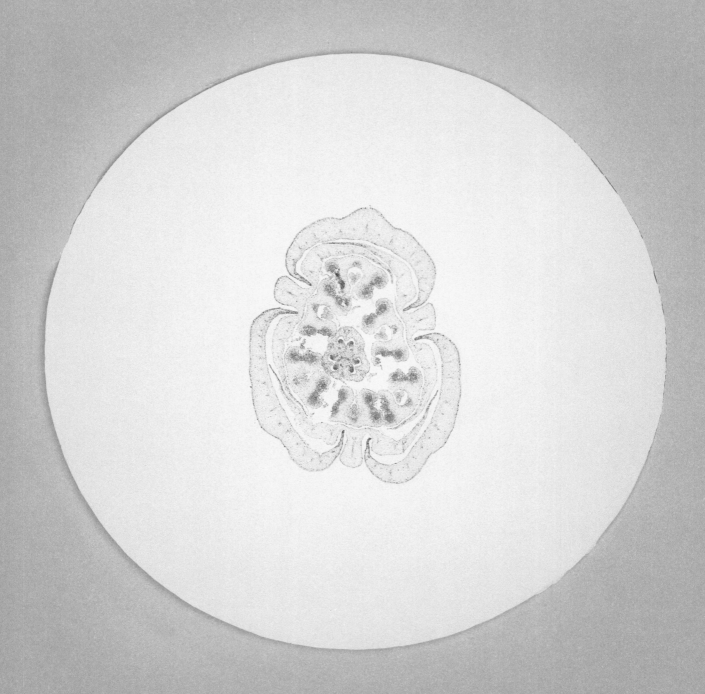

FIG. 06: Meiosis Lilium pollen

FIG. 07: Feather

HOW TO BE AN ESSENTIALIST:

AN INTERVIEW WITH GREG MCKEOWN

In a time when there are more questions than answers, more choices than decisions and more opportunities than hours in a day, many of us are exhausted from trying to do it all. As productive as it makes us feel, pursuing too many things can leave us stressed, anxious and drained instead of turning us into multitasking superheroes. Essentialism: The Disciplined Pursuit of Less *(Crown Business, 2014) is a book that tackles the work-life challenge and provides enlightening pointers on how we can do more with less. We spoke with best-selling author Greg McKeown about worrying less and playing more.*

"The way of the Essentialist isn't about setting New Year's resolutions to say 'no' more, or about pruning your in-box, or about mastering some new strategy in time management. It is about pausing constantly to ask, 'Am I investing in the right activities?' There are far more activities and opportunities in the world than we have time and resources to invest in. And although many of them may be good, or even very good, the fact is that most are trivial and few are vital. The way of the Essentialist involves learning to tell the difference—learning to filter through all those options and selecting only those that are truly essential."
—Greg McKeown, *Essentialism: The Disciplined Pursuit of Less*

WHY DO WE ALL FEEL SO BUSY?
We're in a busyness bubble, which mirrors the real estate bubble of 2008. This happens when there's an overvalued asset (busyness) and a social phenomenon where everybody starts buying into it. There are only two ways out: One is that the bubble will burst, and the other is that we'll see it as a form of madness and get out early. Getting caught up in the busyness bubble isn't sustainable or sensible, and it's not the wise thing to do. So we need to pop it before it bursts.

THERE SEEMS TO BE A HERD MENTALITY THAT SAYS THE BUSIER WE LOOK, THE MORE SUCCESSFUL WE SEEM. WHERE DOES THIS ATTITUDE COME FROM?
I asked someone the other day, "Hi, how are you?" And he said, "Well, we all know the answer now: I'm so busy!" He was so busy that he was averaging four hours of sleep a night for the past two weeks. And he said it with such...

PRIDE?
Pride! He was so happy in his achievement!

HOW CAN WE RECOGNIZE THAT HAVING PRIDE IN OVERWORKING IS FOLLY?

It all starts with us realizing that we've been conned. It's a very persuasive lie: We think that if we can fit it all into our schedules, then we can have anything we want in life. This idea is reinforced in almost every magazine cover we look at and every advertisement we see. It's so pervasive that we don't even notice it exists. So the place to begin isn't even grabbing hold of the Essentialist mind-set—it's recognizing the madness of Everythingism. That's the beginning place. That's when we begin exploring more.

MANY PEOPLE STRUGGLE TO DECIDE WHAT TO SAY YES TO SINCE WE HAVE SO MANY OPTIONS. HOW CAN WE LEARN TO IDENTIFY WHAT IS MOST IMPORTANT TO US?

The options in our lives are increasing faster than our ability to make selections. The choices are exponential, so it's about identifying really selective criteria. To explain this in the book, I use the metaphor of conducting a closet cleanout: When you're trying to purge clothes from your closet, if you use criteria such as "Could I wear this ever again in my life?" the answer is constantly going to be yes. So you end up keeping that item of clothing. But when you employ extreme criteria such as "Do I absolutely love it? Do I wear it often? Does it look great on me?", and if the answer is no, then you should give it away. Now, that's true of closets, but I'm talking about the closets of our lives.

HOW CAN WE GO ABOUT EXPLORING OUR OPTIONS BEFORE CHOOSING THE RIGHT ONE?

An Essentialist explores more options than an Everythingist, but commits to fewer: You're exploring broadly but focusing more sharply and making really selective decisions afterward. As a result, you'll be saying no to a lot more things than the Everythingist does.

I love this line by blogger Derek Sivers: "No more yes—it's either *hell yeah!* or *no*." It's not enough for an opportunity simply to be new, and if you use broad criteria for making decisions such as "Is it interesting?" in a world that has a billion options, you've already set your course: You'll be pulled in and tricked by the trivial. You'll be consumed by the meaningless. But what we want to be able to do is focus on just a few things so we can do truly great work.

I don't think people choose non-essentialism deliberately over Essentialism: People don't say, "I'd rather have 100 average relationships with people I sort of care about instead of four or five meaningful relationships with people I truly love." They choose that course because it happens to be the norm of our times, so they just go along with it. But we never regret an Essentialist choice.

WE OFTEN DON'T REALIZE THAT WE'RE IN CONTROL OF OUR DECISIONS AND DO HAVE CHOICES. WHAT DO PEOPLE MISUNDERSTAND ABOUT THE CONCEPT OF CHOICE?

Right, we're not even pausing long enough to recognize that there *is* a choice! Part of the core mind-set of being an Essentialist is to simply affirm that I have a choice, I can choose, I can make a different choice. Often people logically know that they can choose differently, but emotionally you don't feel that. You feel as if you have a choice, but in all tactical terms you don't—you're living learned helplessness. And in that circumstance, we need to hope that the people who are guiding our lives have our best interests at heart. Because if you don't prioritize your life, someone else will.

WHAT WE CONSIDER ESSENTIAL CAN APPLY TO BOTH TANGIBLE OBJECTS AND INTANGIBLE IDEAS. WHAT'S THE LINK BETWEEN THE PHYSICAL AND EMOTIONAL ESSENTIALS?

I love that question. I recently read Marie Kondo's *The Life-Changing Magic of Tidying Up: The Japanese Art of Decluttering and Organizing*, along with a lot of other people. I love that book! (Turn to page 108 for an interview with Marie.) It's a great place to start. What she's teaching is that, by starting with the most physical purges and then going to the most emotional, you gain confidence over time in discerning between those things. You can build confidence through physically paring down so that eventually you can negotiate which emotional things are important in your life and which things aren't. It's not the only way to learn how to be an Essentialist, but it's one way, and I found it helpful myself.

YOU AND MARIE SEEM TO SHARE AN OUTLOOK THAT ISN'T FOCUSED ON DISCARDING THINGS: INSTEAD IT'S ABOUT DETERMINING WHAT YOU REALLY LOVE, KEEPING THAT AND THEN CUTTING THE FAT AWAY.

Yes, it's important. I really related to that element of her book. I often make the point that I didn't write a book called *No-ism*. The book is *Essentialism*. People should really ask, "What is essential to me?" And then in order to achieve that, "Do I need to give up other things

> "We regret living a life based on other people's expectations of us, and we regret spending too much time at work and not enough time with our family and the key friends in our lives. But we can realign our routines now to celebrate that."

that are less important so I can achieve this?" It's not just less—it's less, but better. Really, people should ask, "What's so important that I'd give up everything in order to achieve it?" When you know the answer to that question, then you have something fantastic. When you're willing to give up those nonessential things— even if they're good, even if they're interesting—that's the beginning.

HOW CAN WE LEARN TO BE BETTER AT PRIORITIZING?
My own personal language discovery for this book was the word *priority*: It came into the English language in the 1400s, and it was singular, because *that's what it means*! It means the first thing, the prior thing, the most important thing. Then ostensibly it stayed singular for the next 500 years, and only in the 1900s did we pluralize the term to *priorities*. What!? What does this word mean now? Can we really have a dozen first most important things? You need to take on whatever that priority is and do it. If you try to do 24 different things simultaneously and treat them all as equally important, you won't get any of them done. And so in that little language change, we can see a lot of how this madness has taken over. It's changing the way we think. It's warped reality.

ESSENTIALISM FOCUSES MAINLY ON REGAINING CONTROL OVER OUR WORK LIVES. YOU'VE CONSULTED WITH A LOT OF BIG COMPANIES. DOES IT GET BETTER OR WORSE NEAR THE TOP?
I first saw the phenomena of Everythingism when I happened to be working with companies like Apple and Google: With their successes came this Trojan Horse of opportunities that undermined the focus that led to their success in the first place. It's this paradox that success can become a catalyst for failure if it leads to the undisciplined pursuit of more, as it often does.

IF WE COULD JUMP FORWARD A FEW DECADES AND LOOK BACK ON HOW WE'RE CURRENTLY PRIORITIZING OUR LIVES, WHAT KINDS OF CHANGES WOULD WE BE MAKING?
If we take the long-term perspective and ask ourselves what we'll regret on our deathbeds, we can extrapolate from that and make different decisions now to prevent having those regrets. We should ask ourselves if our weekly routines currently represent the same values we think we'll wish we'd upheld. We regret basically two things at the end of our lives: We regret living a life based on other people's expectations of us, and we regret spending too much time at work and not enough time with our family and the key friends in our lives. But we can realign our routines now to celebrate that.

HOW MUCH OF THIS IS ABOUT WORK-LIFE BALANCE?
We've all heard this phrase "work-life balance" but it's peculiar because we never say, "Oh, I just need to make sure I'm not spending too much time with my family." But we never mean that when we say we "need to work on our work-life balance." What we mean is, "Am I spending enough time with my family, with my wife? Or am I letting my work consume me?" So we should come up with a more accurate term for the problem we're really trying to solve! It should really be, "I really need to work on my work hours." Or, "I need to make sure that my work isn't the master in my life." *This* is what we're really talking about. And that's why I would emphasize to build an essential routine of an ideal week.

PLEASE TELL US ABOUT YOUR PERSONAL ROUTINE.
I ask myself how I'd ideally like to spend the 168 hours there are in a week. There are three things I hold as a constant design to try and avoid having those regrets on my deathbed [and you'd have to ask my wife how close I get to this]: First, I try to get eight hours of sleep,

because if I don't do that then I can't discern properly, and if I can't discern then I'll get tricked by the trivial. Second, I need 15 hours a week for my wife and I to be together—talking, connecting, going for a walk, going out to eat and so on. Then I'll take 15 hours for my children. Those are my nonnegotiables. You protect those things first. So put those in for you. That accounts for about half of the week. Now out of those remaining hours, what is the best way you could use that time? Since you know you can't solve your problems by just spending more time in the office than anyone else, you have to think smarter. And that space is what being an Essentialist means.

NOWADAYS WE LEAVE VERY LITTLE TIME FOR DOING NOTHING, BUT CREATING THE SPACE TO IMAGINE AND THINK SHOULD BE JUST AS IMPORTANT. HOW CAN WE LEARN TO DO LESS AND PLAY MORE?
I was at the Twitter office a while back, and somebody there said, "Do you remember what it was like to be bored?" (Which I thought was a little ironic, as companies like that are the ones who made us that way!) Every minute we're not actively doing something, we pick up our phones. And what we lose is the concept of play, space, thinking and facing the reality of our lives and the choices we've made.

My own children make me laugh about this subject of creative play and being bored. There are two things I say if my children ever say they're bored: The first is *good*, because I want them to be bored. I want them to have to think about what to do next. I want them to face boredom so they can actually learn how to create, because there's no creativity until there's boredom.

The second thing I say to them if they tell me they're bored is, "That's no problem—I have lots of cleaning you can do! Anytime you're bored, I can give you a task to do." That conversation only needs to take place once! It solves that problem *dead*. And they never say they're bored now. I mean, I have four children—which I know isn't very Essentialist of me—but I see parents all the time who outsource all of their energy to their kids. The parents are now the professional entertainers, and they think it's their job to entertain their kids. Instead, I'm teaching my kids what will be critical for them to do for the rest of their whole lives, which is learning and exploring without being dictated how to be there. And I don't want to steal that from my children.

HOW CAN ADULTS LEARN TO PLAY MORE?
Take email off your phone.

WHEN YOU SAID THAT, I FELT SICK TO MY STOMACH WITH ANXIETY.
Right! When I say this to groups, I ask how many people have email on their phones, and of course every single hand goes up. When you tell them to take it off, you have every single eye in the room on you, because everybody knows that this is jugular. They realize they've been had! This is the great con of our lives. Making your phone more boring will introduce more boredom into your life.

Your email is not a priority tool. That's a lie, because as soon as we really have to be productive, we turn it off. So we know that it's not a productivity tool—it's a communications tool, but it's not even very good for that. If you really need to communicate with somebody, pick up the phone and call them. Email on our phones has to stop! Take all the apps off your phone you don't use and only keep the genuine utility apps. When I first did that, I had withdrawal symptoms. I'd still go to check my phone, but nothing was there—suddenly it was just a boring phone.

We check our phones on average 150 times a day, 900 at the highest levels: That's what we're doing instead of playing, instead of thinking—we're just checking our phones. So we've got to make our phones boring. We can still have them and use them as they have a ton of utility in them, but we have to show them who is boss. Try it for a week!

You don't have to be nuts about this. Essentialism isn't about hiding away up a mountain—though there are worse things you could do than go into monk mode for a while—and I know there are times when having email on your phone is very helpful for a variety of needs. I understand what it's like. We just need to be aware of it and say, "I don't need it now, so it's coming off." This is what Essentialism means: the deliberate, conscious strokes instead of taking it all for granted.

WHAT'S GOING TO HAPPEN TO THE WORLD IF WE DON'T ELIMINATE OUR EVERYTHINGIST MIND-SETS?
Think of it this way: What will a society that never ponders be like? I really wonder about it—what it will be, what we will give up for what we gain. We're being sold on what Everythingism gives us, but we're not being sold on what we're giving up for it.

Greg McKeown is an author, public speaker and former Everythingist. Born in London and now based in Silicon Valley, he spends his time teaching companies how to make better use of theirs.

WORDS
ALICA FORNERET
JESSICA GRAY
JOANNA HAN
RACHEL EVA LIM
GAIL O'HARA

PHOTOGRAPHS
JONAS BJERRE-POULSEN
NICOLE FRANZEN
ALICE GAO
MARTYN THOMPSON
JAN VERLINDE

ILLUSTRATIONS
CHIDY WAYNE

The Essential
Endeavors

For one reason or another, many creative professions involve the art of cutting things down to their essence. In this profile series, we interview a series of designers, editors, authors and entrepreneurs from different fields about how they weave essentialism into their practices.

Jonas Bjerre-Poulsen

We chat with one of the founders of Copenhagen multidisciplinary design firm Norm.Architects about the fundamentals of their creative process.

The team at Danish design firm Norm. Architects believes that buildings and products should incorporate quality materials and be durable and timeless. Designs that meet these requirements will stand the test of time, so they aim to create things that stimulate consumers beyond offering them mere "visual calories." Their design process is based around the idea of asking why a product should be created, and they always try to reach a point where there's nothing to add and nothing to take away that can improve on the item's form and function. We spoke with Jonas Bjerre-Poulsen, who runs the firm with Kasper Rønn von Lotzbeck and Linda Korndal.

How do you keep your creative minds productive and focused as you've developed your skills as graphic designers, art directors and industrial designers? — Architecture typically has a long-term perspective, and we've carried that notion into our ways of thinking about everything, from graphics to photography over to furniture, lighting and industrial design and into interior architecture and styling. We keep focused and productive by constantly pushing each other's ideas and performances forward, and as a result, our designs are taken to a higher level than if we were working separately. Our team works everywhere and all the time. We can't help it and we love it. We don't consider it work but still look at it as a hobby and consider ourselves enthusiasts. It's important to keep that in mind, even though the business is growing.

What's essential to your design process? — We've made it a virtue to focus on quality, durability and timelessness. Design shouldn't just be easily digestible, nor should it be new just to be new. Not only do we want our designs to be made of good materials with good craftsmanship, we want them to embody beauty, history and, most importantly, to outlive fleeting trends. Our process is based on not just asking the question *how?* but asking *why?* Why should we create this? Why does the need for this product exist? Why should people buy it? Why should they want to keep it? When you ask why, you open yourself up to deeper design dimensions and embark on the road to create truly durable products.

How does your background influence your methods and aesthetic? — Keeping in the spirit of the tradition for Scandinavian simplicity, we strive to cut to the bone in our designs. We try to find the simplest shape for a given task without forgetting the beauty of the shape. The Scandinavian tradition is rooted in a sincere devotion to the craft with a strong focus on using good materials and creating designs that last. Products should not only be durable because of good materials and good craftsmanship, but also aesthetically durable in the sense that you can keep looking at them and find them interesting and beautiful as the years roll by. We take pride in our culture and history, and we hope and aspire to create new norms for Nordic design.

Explain the meaning of your term *Soft Minimalism.* — Minimalism isn't a modern style. It's been the norm in many cultures

> "Reduction and perfection have been the main goals for both craftspeople and inventors because avoiding the irrelevant means emphasizing the important."

all over the globe since the beginning of civilization. Reduction and perfection have been the main goals for both craftspeople and inventors because avoiding the irrelevant means emphasizing the important. People sometimes think of architecture and design in terms of added grandness, but it's often the plain or the reduced that's most striking. In our work we aim for a geometrical purity, a simple naturalness and a humble authenticity for a spatial sense of calm and repose. We want to arrive at the maximum of expressivity with the minimum of expression. We try to balance the visual, the tactile and the sensual to create an unusual but harmonious experience. We bridge the masculine and the feminine with an obsessive attention to detail. That's what we mean by Soft Minimalism.

How do you start a creative process? What do you need to keep in mind throughout the life of a project? — Starting a project is all about communication with clients and with each other, no matter if it's architecture or design. In architecture, we must understand people's needs and the way they live—so we have long conversations with the client. We try to adapt to a situation that's not our own. With design, we talk to people who know what it's like to work with certain things. Understanding the key elements about a product or a task is the most important factor in designing.

Where do you find inspiration? — Our inspirations and processes are extremely diverse. We don't have a special formula for gathering inspiration. Sometimes we see an old product and think to ourselves that it's great but that we could improve on the aesthetic or function using new technology. Sometimes a certain manufacturing process, a visit to a factory or a talk with a craftsman inspires us. Sometimes shapes in graphics or ideas in a piece of art inspire us. Sometimes we rationally analyze everyday situations to uncover needs that aren't yet fulfilled by other products in the market. Sometimes an idea just starts out with the fascination of a material or surface, other times we get a precise brief from a producer. But what we think makes us different from many other designers is that we almost never work with our hands. We don't have any hands-on experience with crafts. We have the analytical approach of architects.

Norm.Architects is known for using a specific color palette. Would you consider these colors essential and, if so, why? — There's no denying that we're big fans of using natural colors: the soft beige color of a freshly cut oak tree or the perfect shade of stone gray. These colors are the perfect match for our design. They're timeless. We like to say we work with nuances and not colors. In that sense, I feel we're closely related to Japanese aesthetics.

Would you consider the products you design to be essential household items? — We try to focus on designing objects to fill a need, but sometimes we also design objects that are just aesthetically pleasing— just decorative objects. You could argue that beauty is a need. AF

Photograph on page 103: Part of Norm.Architects' designs for the &tradition showroom. **Above:** As part of their collaboration with &tradition, Norm.Architects designed a cluster of 12 minimalist houses situated within an industrial warehouse on Copenhagen's Paper Island. **Right:** An &tradition Another Rug in Red Volcano, designed by All the Way to Paris.

Marie Kondo

Obsessed with tidying from an early age, Marie has turned decluttering into a full-time job, writing four books and helping others simplify their lives.

Marie Kondo is the author of four books on the art of getting rid of nonessential possessions, including the best-selling *The Life-Changing Magic of Tidying Up: The Japanese Art of Decluttering and Organizing* (Ten Speed Press). She has built her career around helping people scale back the contents of their homes to only contain things that make them truly happy. Her KonMari Method of cleaning emphasizes only keeping items that spark joy and clearing your home of other excess objects. Marie, who has always been besotted with tidying, discusses the psychological benefits of decluttering and how this philosophy extends to other parts of her life.

Is essentialism a part of Japanese culture? — Definitely. Japanese people exhibit a meticulous attention to sensibility, from the way they process ideas to how they approach their surroundings. This is an important aspect of the culture that feeds into essentialism. The idea of *tokimeki*, which represents the foundation of my approach to tidying, is also very Japanese and allows people to reflect on their feelings toward certain objects and ensures that they only keep items they have valuable relationships with. There's also a traditional Japanese expression called *mono no aware* that connotes a sense of empathy and sensitivity to one's surroundings and the impermanence of life itself. By realizing that their presence on this earth is transient, Japanese people are discerning about what they choose to allow into their lives.

What parts of your life could you not live without? — My family, a place to return home to and a notepad or digital note-taking application to write down my ideas.

What does essentialism mean to you? — It's a way of thinking and living that represents an integral part of who I am as a person and how I live my life. Having things orderly and tidy and eliminating clutter allows me to cherish the important things in my life and sparks tokimeki—a sense of joy that makes my heart flutter.

How does essentialism play a role in your methods of tidying? — Essentialism lies at the heart of tokimeki and is my main philosophy regarding my method of tidying up. Choosing items that give you tokimeki means only keeping things that make you happy and elicit positive feelings. These are items that you truly cherish and value rather than those you keep around for purely decorative purposes or just for the sake of it.

How does practicing essentialism in the home affect your clients' lives in other psychological ways? — Decluttering and tidying up frees us of excess and allows us to refocus on what's actually important. Paring things down to the essentials allows my

> **"Decluttering and tidying up frees us of excess and allows us to refocus on what's actually important."**

clients to free their minds—granting space for new ideas and relationships.

What's essential to one person may not be essential to another. How do you help people determine which sentimental objects or mementos are essential to keep in their homes and offices? — I don't set numerical quotas, measurements or an appropriate target number of items that my clients get to keep once the tidying process is over. It doesn't work like that. I keep my personal opinions out of the matter and pose questions from many different angles so that my clients can approach and evaluate the situation from a variety of perspectives. This process is very much about how they think and feel about what's essential and necessary in their lives, which is different for each individual.

What advice would you give to people who find they have trouble maintaining a clutter-free home? — The notion of not being good or effective at tidying is a misplaced preconception that can be easily surmounted by altering the way in which people go about their decluttering process. My book details different angles from which to address clutter—like what you ought to do before starting to tidy up, a standard set of instructions to determine what you should throw out, how to let go of things, the most efficient order in which to go about tidying, and so on. Thinking that tidying is a troublesome process can often discourage people from getting started and prevent them from realizing the renewed sense of freedom and joy that comes with paring things down to the essentials. It helps to approach the act of cleaning your house as an entire lifestyle change rather than a means to an end. This gives depth and meaning to the tidying process and makes it seem like less of a superficial activity.

At times family members can skew or distort our observations of essentialism. How do you encourage people to work around this? — I encourage them to situate their practice of tidying as a very individualized and personal activity that they partake in for their own benefit. This is something that should be practiced alone, as it necessitates that we confront ourselves, our habits and the things we've accumulated in life. Too often we're influenced by what other people think. Worrying about what our family members may be thinking as we cull items and throw away certain objects that we don't have room for in our lives taints the authenticity of the practice.

Many people have the urge to tidy their spaces before tests or big deadlines. Where does this impulse come from? — The impulse to tidy before an exam or a deadline is a sign of the desire to sit down and concentrate, to clear the visual field of clutter and the workspace of all distractions. Alternatively, this can also be an escape or procrastination tool in order to put off getting to the task at hand.

The KonMari Method encourages tidying the home in one fell swoop instead of doing little by little. Why is this so important in achieving a clutter-free home? — A change in tidying habits necessitates a change in overall mind-set. I believe that people who don't see tidying as an essential element of life can change their ways through a radical shock that dramatically changes the awareness of their surroundings. In order to achieve this, it's necessary that the decluttering process happens in a short period of time and uses the correct method in order to attain the maximum visual and psychological impact that will have long-term effects.

Aside from tidying, how does essentialism play into other areas of your life? — I apply the philosophy of tokimeki in many other areas of my life. I choose which activities and relationships to pursue by the amount of joy they bring me and if they make my heart flutter. While I am a social person, I respectfully turn down invites that I'm not too enthusiastic about or interested in. I bear in mind to always make decisions that don't go against my own heart. JG

Vincent Van Duysen

The acclaimed Belgian architect and designer discusses essentialism, his design process and the importance of context.

Vincent Van Duysen has championed a distinctly minimalist aesthetic and is one of the foremost advocates of the modern Belgian style. After getting his start assisting Cinzia Ruggeri and Aldo Cibic at Milan's renowned Ettore Sottsass studio, he founded his own studio in 1990 in Antwerp. Today he employs around 15 collaborators who work on a variety of assignments ranging from commercial spaces to residential units. We speak with him about how he incorporates essentialism into his creative process.

How does the concept of essentialism play a role in your work? How is this reflected aesthetically in your designs? — Essentialism within my work is typically of a monolithic nature, or archetypal in a sense that it has a classic proportion or familiarity. It can

be at once refined, solid and brutal, such as the staircase I designed for the Graanmarkt 13 project, or simple and classical, such as the pottery I created for When Objects Work. If it's airy, then it's usually in connection with nature, like the pool pavilion at the VDC Residence.

What does essentialism mean to you? — It means undoing the clutter and getting to the core, paring back to the bone and achieving authenticity, simplicity and purity.

What characterizes Belgian design, and how has your Belgian background influenced your style? — Belgium has had a rich history of arts and crafts from medieval times to the present. Although there's a strong sense of pride in industries such

as linen and stone craft, what I find difficult about defining a Belgian "style" is that it becomes easily commercialized and reduced to an "export product." Belgium is cosmopolitan in both arts and culture and has a huge breadth of creativity—theater, dance, fashion, art, performance—with participation from many people. I'd say that the Belgian influence in my work is more about this collective individuality than a shared aesthetic or palette.

Tell us about your design process. — It is constant. I'm always designing in my mind, never from a "blank canvas." I enjoy being as observant as possible and have a strongly visual approach. I regularly sit with my team and discuss ideas and directions to achieve a shared vision.

"Essentialism means undoing the clutter and getting to the core, paring back to the bone and achieving authenticity, simplicity and purity."

What elements are crucial to your workflow and creativity? — Every project is different and it's always so important to connect it to its culture. We must also consider the context, location, relationships, program and brief, and this diversity always results in work that's distinctive and tailor-made.

How do you like to begin and end your days? — In the morning I catch up on yesterday's news that I may have been too busy to see and then enjoy a simple breakfast. In the evening I like to briefly read or look through magazines.

When faced with distractions, how do you manage to clear your head? — For me, design is a continuous process. My mind is always working, imagining and connecting.

Exercise, cooking, conversing, walking the dogs—these quotidian aspects of life help to decompress and order the mind.

What elements of life are most important to you? — Eating, sleeping and conversing.

What are some of your essential work tools? — My inspiration comes from travel, conversations, exhibitions, people and everyday life, but my absolute work essentials are my senses.

What's currently on your reading list? — I have a broad range of interests and read widely on art, photography and architecture. Currently I'm enjoying Nicholas Alan Cope's *Whitewash* and Reyner Banham's *Brutalismus in der Architektur*.

What are your essential foods and drinks? — My diet is honest but diverse, and I enjoy foods from different cultures. Some items I like to have on hand are berries, rice milk, small amounts of dairy and cheese, fresh fruit and vegetables, fish, water and wine. And always a carrot-ginger juice.

Why do you do what you do? — There are so many elements to consider, but my interactions and relationships with clients are of utmost importance. I always take a narrative into account when designing. I enjoy being a storyteller because it's not always about pragmatics—it's about soul. Aside from the utilitarian, and with respect to tradition and familiarity, the experience has to have something unexpected and create an emotional connection. JH

Above: The staircase of Vincent's home in Antwerp, Belgium. Right: Vincent's spacious dining room, which is anchored by two Atelier Tables from the St-Paul Home Collection designed by Vincent himself. Artwork by Tadashi Kawamata hangs on the wall.

Kristen Kish

The award-winning chef discusses her obsession with corn, her culinary rituals and her essentialist approach to cooking and life.

Born in South Korea and adopted by a family in suburban Michigan, Kristen Kish had a close relationship with food growing up, which led her to study at Le Cordon Bleu in Chicago. Today, after paying her dues as a line cook and bagging the *Top Chef* crown in season 10, she has become one of the most compelling and closely watched rising young chefs. After stints as chef de cuisine at Stir and Menton—both part of Barbara Lynch's mini-empire of Boston eateries—she recently left to chart her own course and explore her identity as a chef and individual. We chat with her about her essential cooking tips and tricks, the necessary qualities for running a successful kitchen and the importance of carving out quality time to share a meal with loved ones.

What are your essential kitchen gadgets? — Everything starts with great tools. I don't use anything that's gimmicky. My number one tool in the kitchen would be a sharp knife—it doesn't need to be super-fancy, but it does need to be a well-made knife. I particularly like the Japanese style. Next would be a handheld immersion blender. My mom got me one for Christmas years ago and I find myself using it all the time—from emulsifying vinaigrettes to blending soups, or frothing milk for coffee. A great wood or bamboo cutting board is beautiful to look at and helps keep your knife in good shape. Cooking can also be made more convenient by the way you prepare and organize yourself: Line all your chopped-up ingredients on a tray, store it in the fridge and pull it out when you're ready to cook. Keeping your kitchen neat and tidy during the cooking process is far less stressful. And save the plastic take-out containers—I use them to stay organized!

What's essential in your pantry and fridge? — Admittedly, my fridge and pantry look pretty bare. I tend to shop only for what I want to cook for that night or in the very near future since I dine out and travel a lot. Right now, I have kosher salt for everyday seasoning, a pepper mill—freshly ground pepper is a must—grape-seed oil, extra-virgin olive oil, hot sauce, vinegar, fresh citrus, dark chocolate and various condiments. Oh, and chips. Salty snacks are a necessity.

Are there any foods that many people would consider non-essential that you simply couldn't live without? — Chicken fingers and mayonnaise—either together or separate, it doesn't matter.

What techniques or rules have you learned that you consider essential to cooking great food at home? — Knife skills and cooking terminology are the basics. You can't create stunning, amazingly creative dishes without first understanding the hows and whys.

What lessons has your career has taught you about nonculinary aspects of life? — Patience, so much patience. It doesn't come naturally to me, but I remind myself every day. Also that I can't do everything, all the time and by myself. I've had to learn to trust people around me to help me.

What type of cuisine do you find yourself drawn to and why? — I always seem to have a craving for everything at some point. Every five days or so I crave Italian red sauce, it's like clockwork. As a kid I ate stewed tomatoes from the can as a meal—warmed, cold, didn't matter. It was my go-to food in a can, so perhaps that's a nostalgic thing. But the type of food I really gravitate to now is Southeast Asian. I don't normally cook this type of food, but I appreciate it. I'll sometimes attempt it, but I'm happy to leave it to my favorite restaurants: Pok Pok in Brooklyn and Uncle Boons in Manhattan.

Are there any basic skills required to run a kitchen? — Stir has a super-small staff: two front of house and two back of house. It was more of a collaborative effort and it was essential to work as a true team. To this day, it was my favorite job. Menton was much different: I had a staff of around 13, not including the pastry department. There were lots of different types of people who needed different things. I became a chameleon and wanted to make everyone happy. It was completely necessary to be a lot of things to a lot of people, and to say I did it perfectly would be a complete lie. Day to day, job to job, industry to industry, we have to adapt, think on our feet and wear many different hats. There isn't a perfect formula to managing. I did my best to be compassionate, empathetic and understand each individual person—the way they learn, the way they respond to criticism and what their lives are like outside of work. I tried to get to know everyone in a personal way, or listen to anything they wanted to tell me.

Describe some of your essential everyday routines, food-related or otherwise, since leaving Menton. — Before it was wake up,

go to work, go home, sleep and repeat. Right now, the only thing that remains an actual routine is lots of coffee, checking emails and talking to my manager, Tory. From there, it could be anything. I might have time to read a book or I might not have two minutes to myself. It's an odd thing to "un-employ" yourself to only become exponentially busier in so many different arenas. Many chefs these days do this but it's still very new and unexpected for me. I'm figuring it all out as I go while being surrounded with great people, friends and mentors who know more than I do to help guide me along. So my routine is meeting great people, learning new things all the time, making mistakes and working on building a future that I'm proud of.

You seem to gravitate toward cooking simple, clean, refined dishes. Do you subscribe to the philosophy that less is more? — *Less is more* is such a broad idea with so many different definitions. Does that mean fewer ingredients, less fanfare, fewer steps, less of an idea? Overall, I'd say less is more in the sense of not overcrowding your vision and having things that aren't necessary. But sometimes more is more. It tends to change depending on the course, who you're cooking for, what your ingredients are, and so on. It's OK to be gluttonous and go big, as long as you do it in a way that's true to who you are—which is cheesy but so true—it will come off as authentic, and that's what makes food, chefs and ideas so special.

What are some of your favorite ingredients to cook with during the summer? — Corn, hands down, followed by tomatoes and bright herbs—anything really that can be eaten raw or barely cooked. Corn is a nostalgic food for me. When I was growing up in Michigan, there was lots of it—in the backyards of friends' houses, down the highway and in every grocery store. I have fond memories of driving down the highway, hopping out of the passenger seat and running up to the farmers table exchanging $1 for ears of corn. My job was to shuck the ears on the back deck with a brown paper

bag. I can't say this was my favorite task, as the wind would blow the silks and it would stick to my arms and make them itch. But the payoff was well worth it. As a young 60-pound little kid, I could easily put away three or four ears at a time only to go back for more three hours later.

What value can we derive from slowing down and taking the time to share a meal with loved ones? — Honest conversation. It seems simple and we all think we do it, but our days are filled with talking to acquaintances and strangers and, when we get home to the people we care about the most, we think we have no more to give and scroll through Instagram and check emails. I'm guilty of this too. I've started paying more attention to my time with loved ones and talking and sharing time with someone who knows me. It keeps me from getting lost and makes me better for everyone around. Time is extraordinarily valuable and one of the greatest gifts you can give.

Were there any lessons that your parents passed down to you? — My parents allowed me to make my own mistakes, whether they know it or not. They watched from a distance and were there to help me if things got bad but gave me space to make my own decisions. For me, it was invaluable. It was imperative that I mess up so I could appreciate the good and want to do better.

What about your home life? Who do you often share meals with? — My home life used to be just me ordering takeout and watching shitty television. Now the person I share most of my meals with when I'm not traveling is my girlfriend. It's much different than restaurant meals: There's no noise, we sit at the table in sweatpants, T-shirts and no shoes catching up with no distractions. Our meal is often something we've cooked together—though I will say I like it best when I cook and she keeps me company. Cooking is how I show love, and when I can show that to the person I truly adore and share my life with, well, that's just a perfect combination. REL

Lee Ayu

Akha Ama Coffee's cofounder works with farmers from his hometown to cultivate and harvest coffee beans using sustainable techniques.

The first in his village to attend college, Lee Ayu has a commitment to social entrepreneurship that sets him apart from the vast numbers of third-wave coffee purveyors operating in today's society. Through his small-scale approach and deep personal investment in the cause, he has worked tirelessly to improve the lives of farmers in northern Thailand—beginning with the humble coffee bean. We speak with Lee about his work process and some essential life lessons he's picked up along the way.

What element of life is most important to you? — Knowledge. It's one of the most important tools for building sustainability and establishing social equality, and cultural and life skills are necessary for anyone who wants to have an impact on society. It allows me to secure food, shelter, clothing and medicine.

How did growing up in a remote village shape your view of the world? — When I was growing up, my family and I harvested our own rice and vegetables, built our own house and made our own clothing. My family's education came from real life, but I grew up in the school system learning from theory rather than practice. I was taught to be competitive, but my rural life experiences brings me back to my roots. The people in my home village have a very close relationship to nature—we must be aware of the seasonal calendar, which guides our life. I'm very familiar with the slow life.

How is coffee essential to everyday life? — To me, coffee *is* life. It's a bridge to many wonderful things. It wakes you up, provides fuel to drive the day, cultivates friendships and is good for your metabolism!

Please describe the coffee culture in Thailand. What's it like and how has it changed over the years? — There's an abundance of great coffee shops in Thailand, as well as many developing cafés. We're heavily influenced by coffee culture in the West, especially the West Coast of the U.S. and Melbourne, Australia. We have one of the most active coffee cultures in Southeast Asia, and this has all happened in the past five years since Akha Ama was established.

Tell us about your work process. — Time and passion are crucial for me. My work requires that I take small steps and work slowly from the bottom up. It's very important that what we do at Akha Ama Coffee is not about competing as a business, but about creating opportunities for communities to grow. For me, the work is not about money, but about sustainability and social impact.

What inspires you? — My mother. She's one of the strongest women I know, and she taught me to contribute to the world not just by helping people, but also by helping nature and the earth.

Why do you do the work you do? — I grew up with lots of support from the people around me, so I want to give back to society without expecting anything in return. No matter how smart we are and how wealthy of a society we live in, it is meaningless unless we help one another. JH

Rujeko Hockley

While putting together exhibitions at the Brooklyn Museum, this curator has learned that art is essential.

Rujeko Hockley is an assistant curator of contemporary art at the Brooklyn Museum. Her background in cultural studies and interests in social movements and diaspora inform her work in many ways, resulting in a strong commitment to connecting multiple publics to art, artists and scholarship. She believes that art, in all its forms and arenas, is essential.

Is art essential? — Absolutely. In all its forms—writing, music, dance, film—it matters. It can expand our minds, change our views, our understanding of the past, our visions for the future and our empathy for ourselves and others. In a recent TED Talk, the artist Theaster Gates stated that beauty is a service like public education and sanitation, one that we all have a right to. That is really it, the truth.

One of your main objectives is to bring artists together to talk about their work. Why do you think that's important? — Hearing artists talk about what, how and why they make art can be incredibly valuable, for the artists themselves, their community and the general public. There's a certain mystique and mythology around artists, particularly in the broader culture. However, like any of us, they are people at work—trying new things, getting sidetracked, sometimes failing, sometimes succeeding. Hearing from them directly can dispel some of the less interesting elements of this mythologizing, leaving room for the true magic.

When people think of the word *essentialism*, they often think of minimalism. What's the relationship between essentialism and art, and how is that different from minimalism? — For me, the relationship is between essentialism and what we might call "constructed-ness." I see essentialism as problematic: In the abstract, the idea that there's some essence, some fundamental set of attributes integral to a particular group by which you can identify or understand them is benign. In practice, it's an idea that has justified a lot of horror in the world, and its applications have often been limiting and pejorative, and even dangerous—particularly for the least powerful members of a society. Where this intersects with art… well, think about so-called "women's art" or "identity art," and the ways in which those areas are sometimes devalued, deemed less relevant or important because they're not "universal." Which raises the question, *Who or what is universal, and who gets to decide?* There's sometimes a desire for the work made by artists who "fit" certain categories to fulfill or display something essential. To return to this idea of "constructed-ness," I'm more interested in the ways we make and remake ourselves and the work we do than in any "essential" notion of self or practice.

How has your career as a curator affected the way you think about objects in your own life? — I've always been very attached to objects—books, photos or knickknacks—and I've attached meaning to them. I'm very particular about how they're placed or interacted with. Perhaps being a curator has made me think more carefully about what I bring into my home. AF

Matt Dick

We talk to the Small Trade Company founder about working with a diverse group of makers in the San Francisco area.

Matt Dick founded the clothing and product business Small Trade Company in 2010 in the Bay Area. Although he has a background in fashion design and styling, he never anticipated that he would end up designing work uniforms, one of the company's featured products. Matt speaks with us about how he's discovered through his work that there's a purpose behind considering how every aspect of our lives is thoughtfully consumed or navigated.

What kind of products do you create, and who do you create them for? — We create products for anyone, not for everyone. I really believe that things get better with age. How you live with what you buy is very important—not everyone has time to learn from what they consume, but if you can, then you begin to manifest something special. Nothing is guaranteed for life— sometimes the more fragile the better. We create products across the spectrum,

mostly something to pass on, mend and keep. We believe in what we make and who we do business with.

What are some basic design procedures you apply across the board to any piece of apparel? — I still stand with form follows function, and our designs always begin with the search for fabric. I love design—it's one of the best moments of humanity.

Could you tell us a little about some of your more recent design work? — The current collection we did is based on the kurta, a men's work shirt from India. Even outside of the workwear we make to order, our designs are based on people working somewhere.

What were you doing before you started Small Trade Company? — I came from a school that taught me to dissolve boundaries around the arts and design. I consider that to be the foundation of my company

without parameters, and it's the only commitment to our endeavor at hand.

What makes work clothes essential? — People read what you put on or how you dress in relation to your environment before you have a chance to speak. Our company is rooted in collaboration and our work is part of a space and the people moving in that space. It's part of the passing on of the story I tell with clothing.

What makes an item of clothing essential to its wearer? — Something being essential depends on its owner, so I feel that's out of my hands.

Is there any semblance of work-life balance at Small Trade Company, or is it all "do what you love, love what you do"? — As long as my eyes are open, I guess no. But my other occupation is sleeping—at any time of the day—because we work into the night. AF

Above: Small Trade Company's work studio in San Francisco, California. Right: A mood board that helps keep Matt and his fellow designers creatively energized and inspired.

Katherine Connor Martin

The head of U.S. dictionaries at Oxford University Press talks about the importance of choosing the right words.

Few people understand the importance of cutting something down to its very essence more than good writers and editors, and who better to discuss the art of editing, word selection and getting back to basics than the editors who work on the dictionary? Katherine Connor Martin leads an editorial team that researches, drafts and edits American English entries in the historical *Oxford English Dictionary* and the contemporary dictionary website. She offers some insight on what it means to make sure the dictionary is correctly edited, well presented and contains no unnecessary nonsense.

How does the concept of essentialism play a role in the work that you do? — Editing down to the essentials is at the core of lexicography [the practice of compiling dictionaries]. At the research stage, lexicographers look at all of the available evidence for a word's use, and then determine what the essential, core meanings are. Then in defining these meanings in usually a single sentence, we must ruthlessly strip away extraneous details and home in on the crucial information needed to convey the meaning to the reader.

Describe the process of culling the *Oxford English Dictionary* (OED). How many people are involved in working on it? What does it take to add or remove a word from it? — The OED has dozens of full-time editors and researchers and hundreds of consultants. The second edition of the dictionary [running to 20 print volumes] was published in 1989, and we are now engaged in the mammoth task of revising the entire dictionary. Words are never removed from the historical OED, because it aims to cover the full history of English. Even if a word is no longer used, it

remains in the dictionary. Thousands of new words and senses are added each year. The vocabulary of English is constantly growing and changing, so we always have more to do. Even in smaller dictionaries than the OED, one of the great benefits of digital dictionaries is that we don't have to remove entries for the sake of space. If a word has become rare in contemporary English, people still might encounter it in books, and the dictionary should be able to give them information about it.

Did you read dictionaries growing up? How did you find your way into this line of work? — I enjoyed studying languages and history, so I always had a lot of dictionaries. When I was in college, I requested and received a single-volume microprint edition of the OED as a Christmas gift: It has 12 tiny pages printed on each page, and you need a magnifying glass to read it. Today's

> "With each dictionary entry we draft or revise, we add in some small way to the sum total of human knowledge."

students are lucky to be able to access it through the website instead. So I was a big OED fan, but it never occurred to me that working for the OED was a possible career path. I saw a listing for a lexicographer position at Oxford University Press completely by chance—I actually had to look up the word lexicographer, because I didn't know what it meant—and thought, "that sounds like the perfect job for me."

What does essentialism mean to you? — There are two main strands to the meaning of *essential*: "absolutely necessary or extremely important" on the one hand, and "fundamental or central to the nature of something or someone" on the other. So for each individual, there are things that are essential to her as a person [say, power and recognition] and qualities that are essential aspects of her character [ambition]. Obviously, these are interconnected—you can learn a lot about someone by finding out what's important to them.

What are some of your work essentials, including actual tools or sources of inspiration? — The classic image of an OED lexicographer is a bearded James Murray in his scriptorium, surrounded by the millions of paper slips that were used to produce the first edition of the OED. Many people are surprised that today's lexicography is a digital affair. The key tools are historical databases that can be mined for evidence and huge corpora of billions of words that are analyzed using special software. Dictionaries are written using XML editors and content management systems. I love working digitally, and I'm not a fetishist of the printed page. However, there are certain types of thinking that I do best with a pen in my hand. I always have a good gel ink pen with me, and when a definition gets particularly thorny, I turn away from the screen and write things out. I also take notes in longhand—not because I actually plan to look back at them, but because the act of writing helps me to commit things to memory. I often just write on whatever scrap paper is at hand and recycle it immediately

afterward. The other thing I have to have on paper is a calendar. The functionality of digital calendars is far superior, but I have a mental block—I can't work with deadlines and schedules unless I have a printed calendar to look at.

Do you struggle with any constant distractions from your work? Have you come up with any good methods for keeping yourself focused? — Yes! Email is a terrible distraction, especially because of the asynchronicity—you end up waiting for each other's responses and days go by before you can act. I try to have live conversations in person or over the phone whenever possible, and having the majority of my colleagues in the UK brings an unexpected benefit: I have far fewer disruptions after noon, when their workday ends.

Are there any food or drink essentials that you like to keep in your home or office? — Maldon salt. I sprinkle a little bit on everything, including chocolate.

Do you ever keep certain things handy in case of emergency? — I'm not so frivolous as to consider putting sea salt in my go-bag, but I will admit to sometimes taking a box with me when I go on vacation.

When you strip away the excess, what elements of life do you consider to be most important? — Spending time with friends and family, learning new things and good food with good company.

At the end of the day, why do you do what you do? — Samuel Johnson famously defined *lexicographer* as "a harmless drudge." It's true that the work I do is painstaking and not infrequently tedious. But there has never been a day when I didn't learn something new, which is very important to me. And it's a privilege to contribute to a great reference work like the OED: With each entry we draft or revise, we add in some small way to the sum total of human knowledge. That's a good reason to get out of bed in the morning. GO

Lisa Hedge

The cofounder of Venamour stationery talks about her design process, simplicity and essentialism.

Lisa Hedge first began her studies at the University of Southern California intent on pursuing studio arts. There, she was introduced to the world of graphic design and redirected her path to develop a career as an art director and designer. After finishing school, she interned at Takashi Murakami's New York art studio, developed her free-lance career and worked with clients including Warby Parker and L'Oréal. Today, the New York–based designer continues to call on her arts background as one half of the Venamour stationery design team. She discusses the essential elements of her work from inspiration to creation.

How would you articulate the difference between essentialism and simplicity when it comes to design? — There's definitely a relationship between the two, but it seems that it would depend on both intention and context. I think of simplicity as aesthetic minimalism and essentialism as an ideal that subjects all decisions about style to the necessity of function. Despite the inclination to link the two, something can be decidedly not simple—elaborate, ornamental, messy or mysterious—and more effectively serve its purpose. For me, part of the pleasure of design is the license to experiment with style as a way of making something more persuasive and engaging, and hopefully more essential by default.

In what ways does negative space work to highlight a main article of focus? — Negative space doesn't really factor itself into the decision-making process consciously for me. When your attention is on the subject, such as folded paper or the product to be showcased in an ad, you're considering all elements of the space while working toward a balanced composition with a point of focus. My paper landscape project was a playful study where I used shadows to draw and redraw a sense of space within the picture plane, and Target's Threshold campaign featured a series of interior vignettes, each with an element of fantasy that bridged interior and exterior space.

When you are working with the medium of collage, how do the essential components fit together to express a larger but cohesive concept? — I love that collage is all about spontaneous relationships, a process that's evident in the finished work. With my floral collages, elements are tied together through a coherent style, despite how they might be reshuffled from one composition to another. Whether the glue is conceptual or purely visual, the randomness of collage somehow enables a visual logic that can't be premeditated.

How does essentialism affect your commercial work as well as graphic design for invitations? — No matter who the the client is or what kind of project we're working

> —
> "I think of simplicity as aesthetic minimalism and essentialism as an ideal that subjects all decisions about style to the necessity of function."

on, I'm always hoping to create work that's thoughtful and intelligent. Things would be rather lackluster, however, if we didn't make room for the playful, irreverent, ephemeral, excessive and impractical pleasures that also have their place. At Venamour, we always consider both what's explicitly essential to making an invitation useful (language, clarity, legibility) and what makes it beautiful and desirable—qualities that are less tangible but equally valid.

Where did your inspiration for the Wildflower Collection come from? — When my sister got married in the garden of our family home in California, the day existed as a hazy daydream in our minds before the fact—as is the case with so many weddings. The process of designing the Wildflower Collection began when I was there, with her vision of the events and a shortlist of flowers. There would be garden roses, afternoon sun, the scent of rosemary and salt water, bare feet, lush color, soft whites and overall a loose formality tied together with a romantic and no-fuss sentiment. Translating that into a design was entirely an experiment, but it came together through illustration, collage and some organized typography to suit her practical nature.

Is your unadorned design aesthetic reflected in your personal life or style? If so, how? — I wish I could say so. Maybe we reinvent ourselves through our work, to make things neat and orderly where our personal lives are not. I'd love to say it's all a cohesive package, but organized chaos is maybe the unspoken mantra of my workspace. When it comes to my life outside of work, as a new business owner I'm looking forward to reclaiming one of those at some point. It's currently a work in progress!

How did you end up working with Takashi Murakami? What was that experience like and in what ways did his busy style influence the way you think about design? — When I first moved to New York, I interned at his studio and it was a brief but memorable experience. I was contributing to an immense paint-mixing effort, and it was a lesson in color theory of epic proportions. It was really interesting getting to participate in a small community of artists, all working to bring a particular work of art to fruition.

What do you consider to be the most important personal items in your own life? — I think it would have to be items that have stories tied to them that keep me inspired: books inscribed with personal notes, furniture crafted by loved ones, that sort of thing. I still even keep notes and charcoal sketches from certain classes from my days as a student at the University of Southern California. Even when they are tucked away, I keep them as a reminder to keep learning and drawing. AF

Above: Laid out on the desk are some paper goods from Lisa's Wildflower, Botanical and Viridian collections. **Right:** Some of Lisa's inspirations on display at her studio in Clinton Hill, Brooklyn.

WORDS
JULIE POINTER

PHOTOGRAPHS
KATHRIN KOSCHITZKI

Traces of Summer

There's too much freedom to be embraced on the most successful dog days to fret over cleanliness or perfect presentation, even if that means leaving the house with unmade beds, watermelon rinds piled on the front porch and grass-stained clothing.

These longed-for days of cricket calls invite us to pare away those superficial worries that can make us tense the rest of the year. Instead, our essential focus can turn to wringing the most out of every light-filled day.

Through this return to childlike simplicity, we start to reconsider the most essential joys in life, such as the love of the one sharing our sandy sheets, salty unkempt hair, stacks of guacamole-encrusted bowls and the privilege to play.

A well-spent summer should leave its residue everywhere. Beach blankets piled in the backseat form miniature sand dunes. Shoulders boast mosquito welts and fingers carry scratches from wild berry picking. Forgotten freckles reappear and the boldest tan lines are flaunted.

This summer, remember friends from times past and celebrate fresh memories being made.
Try to forgo your normal sense of propriety in order to make space for praising the grand
gesture that this season is, no matter how rumpled and wild it may leave us.

WORDS
SARAH BAIRD

PHOTOGRAPHS
NICOLE FRANZEN

The Most Essential Oil

Praised for centuries as both an ailment-curing liquid gold and a simple foundation for many cuisines, olive oil is one of the most essential ingredients in the Mediterranean and beyond. This photo essay pays tribute to the enduring fruit that gives so many cultures reasons to gather and enjoy meals together.

My childhood friend's Cyprus-born grandfather once recalled an old adage as we ran among the olive trees at her family's farm: "If you fall asleep under a fig tree, you get a headache," he said. "But if you fall asleep under an olive tree, you dream."

Olives have long been the fruit of visionaries and dreamers, ever since Athena stood over Athens with a peaceful olive branch in hand. Long before it became a staple in modern pantries, olive oil was exalted in ancient religious texts: It's one of the first foods mentioned in the Hebrew Bible, Muhammad deemed olive trees holy in the Koran, it's daubed on baptized heads in Judeo-Christian tradition and its branches were found in the Tutankhamen tomb to protect the pharaoh in the afterlife. As long as there have been societies, there have been olive trees. And as long as we've had these symbols of beauty and resilience, we've had olive oil.

This thimble-size fruit wields unlimited power in many contemporary cultures and has long been the gastronomic bedrock of Western civilization. It's a simple addition to countless meals and forms the foundation for cooking in the Mediterranean and beyond. Though groves can now be found all over, Spain, Italy and Greece lead the way in production. The most serious consumers are the Greeks—each citizen allegedly slurps upward of an overwhelming 25 liters (nearly 7 gallons) a year.

The obsession goes beyond the edible, especially in these nations' superstitions: Italians believe that if you spill olive oil you must dabble it behind your ear to ward off bad luck; Greek tradition dictates that if olive oil is dripped into a bowl of water and sinks, an "evil eye" is afoot; and there's the all-peaceful olive branch itself, which Sicilians hang from their chimneys to keep lightning away. It's also been a lynchpin of beauty rituals from the past and present—ever since the Minoans of 3500 BC used oil as cleanser instead of soap, we've found ways for it to smooth our hair, perfume our bodies and make our skin glow.

"Olive people have something special about them," says Mort Rosenblum, an olive grove owner and author of *Olives: The Life and Lore of a Noble Fruit.* "It's this tribe of people who really love the plant that's oiled the wheels of civilization for 10,000 years." Olive oil binds families together, particularly during the annual harvest. Small farms often host a homecoming celebration when far-flung cousins, daughters and sons come home to lend a hand.

In this way, olive oil has become more than just a pantry staple: It's a balm of folklore and kinship, the ointment of the people and a symbol of staying grounded in tradition. Some Greek farmers even claim they can trace the deep, knotted roots of their still-living trees back more than 2,000 years.

Standing strong not just through generations but centuries, olive trees become landmarks, reminders of the past and what can become of the future. Firmly planted in the earth, resilient and respectful of their place in history, they reflect the communities and people who invest in them.

SERVES 8

OLIVE OIL CAKE
WITH BLOOD ORANGE ZEST

After a recent trip to California's olive groves, James Beard Award–winning chef Michael Anthony (executive chef at Gramercy Tavern and Untitled at the Whitney) reconnected with his Italian heritage to put a citrus-infused spin on a traditional olive oil cake.

Nonstick cooking spray

2 ¼ cups (255 grams) unbleached cake flour

1 tablespoon baking powder

¼ teaspoon salt

1 ¾ cups (385 grams) full-fat Greek yogurt

1 ¼ cups (250 grams) sugar

3 large eggs

½ cup (120 milliliters) California extra-virgin olive oil, plus more for brushing

Zest of 1 orange, preferably blood orange

½ cup (70 grams) sliced almonds

Crème fraîche, yogurt or jam, for serving

Preheat the oven to 325°F (165°C), and grease an 8 ½-by-4 ½-inch (21.5-by-11-centimeter) loaf pan with nonstick cooking spray. Cut a piece of parchment paper to line only the bottom of the pan.

In a large bowl, sift together the cake flour, baking powder and salt. In another bowl, whisk together the yogurt, sugar, eggs, oil and orange zest. Add the dry ingredients to the wet, and mix with a rubber spatula just until combined but with some small lumps remaining (over-mixing your batter may result in a tough consistency).

Pour the batter into the prepared pan and sprinkle the top with the almonds. Bake until a wooden skewer inserted in the middle of the cake comes out clean and the cake springs back when lightly pressed, 45 minutes to 1 hour. Cool completely, then run a dull knife around the edges of the pan before removing.

To serve, cut the cake into 1-inch (2.5-centimeter) slices, lightly brush both sides with olive oil, and toast under a broiler until lightly browned. Serve with a dollop of crème fraîche, yogurt or jam.

JAN SØNDERGAARD
1930S FISHERMAN'S HOUSE
SJÆLLAND, DENMARK

WORDS
RACHEL EVA LIM

PHOTOGRAPHS
WICHMANN + BENDTSEN

Home Tour:
Natural Habitat

Feeling connected to nature is an integral part of life, but it doesn't have to be something we need to leave our houses to experience. We explore a minimal summer home in Sjælland, Denmark, that has mastered indoor-outdoor living, beautiful interior plant life and wide-open spaces.

When the sun shines bright during Copenhagen's precious summer months, Jan Søndergaard heads out of the city to spend some time among the trees. The architect owns a black box-shaped house in Sjælland (a forested island peninsula in Northeast Denmark) that he initially bought at a bargain from a homeowner in Copenhagen. After transporting the entire unit to Sjælland by truck and laying down 24 concrete piles into his plot of land, Jan set to work renovating the house into a place he could call his own. "I spent a good two years expanding and restoring this house with my own two hands and didn't use any electrical tools," he says. "It gradually transformed from a little romantic cottage into a more spacious and livable space." Jan chose to install large untreated windows to allow uninterrupted views of the surrounding forests and maximize the amount of light entering the space. He also constructed a curved ceiling to soften the angles where

the sunlight penetrates the property. "One of my preoccupations as an architect is crafting a space to accommodate light in the best and most efficient way possible," Jan says. "That's part of the identity and character of the Scandinavian people— we seem to have a feel for how to shape space in accordance with natural light." The house's northeast-facing location provides picturesque views of the sunrise, and he takes frequent evening walks along the shore to experience the sun setting along the horizon. "The surface of the water is always lit up by light," Jan says. "I leave the windows open and wake up to the sun shining straight into the center of the house, which is fantastic." As Jan's summerhouse is a mere 1066 square feet (100 square meters) in size, he's selective about what he allows inside, especially as the space occasionally doubles as his work studio. "The less I have around me, the easier it is to form thoughts," he says. "I can think, draw

and look forward to the future instead of always hanging in history." Jan loves living so close to the water and enjoys going on solo fishing trips in his small boat. He often invites his friends from Copenhagen to the house for casual meals, as the warm summer weather allows them to dine outside on a feast of seasonal produce and Jan's catch of the day. "My favorite part of being here in the summer is spending time with my good friends," he says. "We spend long afternoons sitting in the shadows of the trees—eating lunch, drinking wine and taking dips in the sea." After spending most of the year living and working in the heart of Copenhagen, Jan's second home is a peaceful sanctuary and a welcome reprieve from city life. "The house is in a beautiful area that's rather secluded, with the trees acting as natural barriers that section you off from your neighbors," Jan says. "It's a very peaceful place and feels like living in the countryside, which I like very much."

Left: The table was custom built for Jan's home by his longtime friend, the carpenter Jesper Nielsen.
Above: A Rais fireplace sits in Jan's living room, along with handmade shelves that store everything from books to kitchenware. "I'm currently reading a great book about Michael Gottlieb Bindesbøll, perhaps the first modernist of Denmark," Jan says.

Above: Jan's large window frames are made out of wood and reinforced with aluminum on the exterior. Right: The forested area near Jan's house that leads to the ocean. "The water lies on the other side of the trees, and I like sitting in the clearing and enjoying the views for hours," he says.

WORDS
DANIELLE DEMETRIOU

PHOTOGRAPHS
HIDEAKI HAMADA

PRODUCTION
TINA MINAMI DHINGRA

Neighborhood: Yanaka

While so much of Tokyo is in constant motion and blazing brightly, the calm district of Yanaka manages to slow the pace of city living while honoring old-world traditions and welcoming modern ideas.

A gray cat slinks past a wooden house. Two elderly ladies in indigo headscarves sell rice crackers at an old glass counter. A young cobbler slices through a piece of mustard leather in a tiny shoemaking atelier. It's a sunny Friday morning in early spring, and these snatched moments are unfolding in a quietly humming neighborhood that appears to be the antithesis of 21st-century urban life. Judging by the peaceful atmosphere, unrushed residents and leisurely tempo, you'd never guess that this setting is hidden in the shadows of one of the most fast-paced cities on the planet: Tokyo.

Few cities are as strongly defined by their bustling reputations as Tokyo. Simply hearing the name of the sprawling Japanese capital is likely to evoke images of cloud-brushing skyscrapers, neon billboards, trend-triggering teen tribes and a sea of salarymen. But there's one corner of Tokyo where all urban stereotypes dissolve and life moves at a less predictable rhythm: Yanaka, an old-fashioned neighborhood that sanctifies a slower pace of life.

Yanaka's location in eastern Tokyo falls within the central confines of the JR Yamanote train line that encircles the city, yet despite its metropolitan setting, it inhabits a different world entirely from elsewhere in the capital. Here, atmospheric leafy lanes are filled with elderly bike-riding residents, well-preserved wooden houses, exquisite temples and multigenerational family businesses alongside a growing community of young creatives. (Not to mention its cats:

The neighborhood is famed for its wild feline population, with countless cats happily going about their daily business among their human neighbors.)

Yanaka is a textbook example of *shitamachi*, a Japanese word that goes far beyond its literal meaning of "downtown" to evoke the nostalgia of the tightly knit working-class neighborhoods of Tokyo's postwar years. In a similarly old-school vein, Yanaka successfully functions as a self-contained community, thanks to its array of specialty shops, such as tofu makers, rice sellers and green tea merchants, which all still thrive thanks to the absence of big-name chains.

Yanaka owes its special ambience to several historical happenings: Unlike vast areas of Tokyo, the neighborhood survived both the destruction of the 1923 Great Kantō Earthquake and the bombing blitz of the 1945 US air raids. After being spared from these devastating events, a high concentration of temples were added to the neighborhood (dozens were relocated to Yanaka following a 17th-century fire that wiped out much of the city), which cemented its status as an area with a truly unique cultural heritage.

It may have been this atmosphere of architectural preservation—rare in a city with a famously hyperactive skyline—that contributed to Yanaka becoming a hub for craftspeople. This creative spirit lives on today with young Tokyoites continuing to be drawn to Yanaka's community of makers, intimate atmosphere, comparatively

1 Kayaba offers warm beverages and hot buttered toast to visitors stopping in after a visit to SCAI the Bathhouse gallery, which is just around the corner.
2 SCAI the Bathhouse was renovated into a gallery in 1993 after standing as one of Japan's public bathhouses for 200 years.
3 The calm streets of Yanaka make for a beautiful backdrop for early morning strolls to and from the market.

1

2

3

low rents and a slower and more rewarding pace of life.

Among those seduced by Yanaka's charms is Ichiro Kanai, who recalls with near-evangelical clarity the moment he first stumbled upon the area while out cycling 11 years ago. "I saw something very different from anywhere else in Tokyo that day," he says. "It felt very unusual and special—the sky was wide and open, and there was a sense of the familiar that took me back to when I was a child. It felt as though I'd been here a long time before."

Marking a turning point in his life, Ichiro moved from his home near the neon glare of the Shibuya district to Yanaka, where he set up tokyobike, a company that makes simple urban bicycles. Its pared-down design and functional concept draws

on the spirit of Yanaka, and the company's sleek, rainbow-hued frames have since become cult favorites with seven international stores from New York to Berlin.

But tokyobike's headquarters—and its heart—remain in Yanaka. Here, the main store is housed in an atmospheric 80-year-old former liquor store where bike frames are showcased behind a wooden facade and an old tiled roof. "People don't walk very fast in Yanaka like in other places in Tokyo. They even ride their bikes a bit more slowly," Ichiro says. "Basically they aren't in a rush: They eat slowly and they enjoy life. There's also a very strong sense of community. We're friendly and open-minded here. It may be an old town with a storied history, but it's very accepting of new things and new people. The community attracts

young creative types—this slow and open quality allows them to take their time to create beautiful things."

Another one of Yanaka's appeals is that many businesses that have been passed down through generations are still alive and well. Several are found within the retro confines of Yanaka Ginza, a narrow, lantern-lined shopping street known as a *shotengai*.

Included on this list of family businesses is Maruhatsu Fukushima Shoten, a fishmonger that first opened its doors 80 years ago where locals can pick up shellfish and freshwater fish. Musashiya, which has been open since 1923, is another essential pit stop that offers tubs of handmade tofu, and Echigoya Honten, a shop specializing in sake, opened 110 years ago

2

3

and is now operated by fourth-generation owner Toshihiro Honma. "Yanaka's location is very special and hasn't changed for at least 30 years—maybe that's the charm," Toshihiro says. "It's getting quite popular these days. Perhaps it's because it reminds everyone of the local shotengai they went to with their families as children."

The Suzuki family is the third generation to run the nearby 80-year-old Niku no Suzuki. Customers line up daily for its famed *menchi katsu*, a luscious breaded beef cutlet that melts in the mouth and is made with a secret spice blend. When asked how many of these are sold daily, the answer is typically Yanakan: "No one keeps track of that," Mrs. Suzuki says, laughing. "I suppose it all depends on the weather: On rainy days we don't sell as many, but

on sunny ones more customers come, so we sell more!"

The art supply store Tokuouken is another Yanaka landmark. The century-old space is home to one of the few shops in Japan that specializes in pigment paints used in traditional *Nihonga* artwork and has customers ranging from art students to contemporary artists such as Takashi Murakami. The shop's walls are lined with more than 300 bottles of different colored powder pigments, each made from careful blends of minerals, shells and rare stones. "Many Nihonga painters lived in Yanaka in the past," explains fourth-generation owner Yukiko Miyauchi. "Today, mainly art students and artists come here. The paints are difficult to use, so only people who know about them visit."

But everything in Yanaka isn't old-school. One relative newcomer is Atelier de Florentina, a calm, minimal bakery set up by former food writer Mihoko Kajiwara. She first opened a tiny space on Yanaka's Snake Lane in 2010 before moving to Yanaka Ginza several years ago. Today, she bakes half a dozen different types of Florentine cookies a day in flavors such as yuzu and baked apple. She believes that the allure of the area is multifaceted, from the "warm air" that flows through Yanaka's lanes to the locals' respect for small businesses and handmade products. "We love this area so much," she explains. "Yanaka is not just an old town—it also has a mixed culture and a variety of faces. It's an art town, a temple town, a tourism town, a writer's town. Instead of large chain shops,

1   Mihoko Kajiwara and her husband, Makoto, offer special Florentine cookies at their shop Atelier de Florentina.
2   The old-school snack shop known as an *okakiya* is typical of the Yanaka neighborhood.
3   A selection of well-made clothing stocks the Classico showroom.

1

2

there are lots of attractive individual stores. It's all about small places, handmade products and communication."

Hajime Sonoda, a talented shoemaker who runs a small boutique that painstakingly handcrafts leather shoes from scratch, echoes the same sentiments that Mihoko expresses. Like many of the best things in Yanaka, his shoes are made quietly and slowly using quality craftsmanship, soft leathers and a self-described "modern vintage" aesthetic. His customers travel from far and wide, and they not only have impeccable taste but also patience: A single pair can take up to eight months to be completed from the first fitting to final delivery. "We have a good sense of community in this area," he says. "We greet

each other and have brief conversations every morning when local people pass by. We sometimes also gather for dinner or invite people to our atelier for *nabe* hot pot."

This lack of pretension among residents—usually found in rural communities rather than hyper-modern cities—filters down to the local businesses. One such example is a design boutique called Classico. Set on a quiet green lane in two simple rooms that seem more like a home than a retail space, the store showcases humble, functional items for everyday living from stationery and toothbrushes to ceramics and basic clothing. Owner Ryu Takahashi is unwaveringly clear about the type who is drawn to the area: "It's for people who

have their own sense of style. Many specialty shops are scattered throughout residential areas here. Individual owners are able to represent what they like in their own way."

While Yanaka is clearly handcrafted heaven, its appeal goes far beyond shopping. Home to many tiny blink-and-you-miss-it gastronomical gems, Yanaka also celebrates the art of good eating (without rushing, of course).

Some swear by Lemon no Mi, where visitors wait in line to sit at a wooden counter and eat whatever homemade dish the owner Maiko fancies making that day. Other hungry locals make a pilgrimage to Tabi Bagel, a tiny bakery filled with an exotic selection of bagels. Hagiso, a house

3

converted into an atmospheric café and gallery, is another popular lunch spot, and locals also swoon over the steaming bowls of soba noodles washed down with sake at Takajo.

In addition to being spoiled with both food and shopping options, Yanaka's residents have something else to celebrate: an impressive community spirit that casts an invisible link between everyone in the area. Ask any newcomers about their experiences here and they'll name a number of residents or businesses that have been especially kind and supportive.

One person who knows all about this open spirit is Masami Shiraishi, the president of one of Yanaka's most inspirational landmarks: SCAI the Bathhouse,

an independent art gallery housed in a 200-year-old former bathhouse. Here, beneath a charmingly curved tiled roof and towering chimney, exhibitions by world-class artists such as Anish Kapoor, Lee Ufan and Tatsuo Miyajima are regularly showcased.

Masami is a pioneer in the area: He opened his gallery in 1993 and more recently renovated the generations-old coffee shop Kayaba just around the corner. He continues to play an active role in the community today—his latest project involves transforming three abandoned houses into a bakery, beer hall and small market. "Yanaka has a close-knit community with intimate local interaction," he says. "People greet one another across narrow

residential streets and many traditional manners are still being practiced. Much of Tokyo's cityscape has lost its original charm, but those charms have been kept intact in this neighborhood. And it's conveniently located within the Yamanote line, so it's not even in suburban Tokyo."

But the ultimate endorsement for Yanaka can perhaps be echoed by some of its most populous residents: the cats. As Mihoko from Atelier de Florentina muses with a smile: "Cats have always been drawn to quiet, peaceful neighborhoods. They know that in Yanaka they'll be safe and find food. They basically understand that it's the nicest place to live in Tokyo." And cats don't get that kind of thing wrong.

Kinfolk
Gatherings

Chef Alice Waters once noted that "the power of gathering is that it inspires us, delightfully, to be more hopeful, more joyful, more thoughtful: in a word, more alive." We'd like to continue welcoming new readers and friends to our events around the world.

PHOTOGRAPHS
Above: Lisbon, Portugal: Rodrigo Cardoso—
De Alma e Coração
Right: Brooklyn, New York: Karen Mordechai

Kinfolk explores concepts and ideas related to the Slow movement by building experiences that examine life's essential qualities. This year, we've added different types of events to our international gatherings series, including film screenings, panel discussions and workshops that explore how we can build collaborative relationships with our fellow entrepreneurs, makers and creatives. We won't be abandoning our beloved long table dinners, of course, but we aim to continually incorporate a diverse range of experiences that explore our core values in new ways. We hope you can join us to slow down, spend more time with friends, family and neighbors and actively participate in the simple but profound act of gathering around a table.

We're so grateful to all of our hosts, partners, collaborators and attendees who embody the values we hold so dear.

Kinfolk gatherings will continue through 2015 across the globe. For information on upcoming locations, tickets and other details, please keep an eye on our events page.

www.kinfolk.com/events

Event-related inquiries, comments and simple "hellos" are warmly welcomed at: community@kinfolk.com

ISSUE SIXTEEN CREDITS

SPECIAL THANKS

*Thanks to Katrin Coetzer for the Starters
and Essentials illustrations*

ON THE COVER

Photographer Neil Bedford
Styling Rachel Caulfield
Hair Marcia Lee
Makeup Crystabel Riley
Model Nadja at Elite Models London
Casting Simon Lewis at Cast and Elect
Production We Are Up Production

Clothing Shirt by Joseph; hat by Reiss

THE ESSENTIAL NON-ESSENTIALS

Photographer Mikkel Mortensen
Styling Lene Rønfeldt
*Special thanks to LYNfabrikken
for the location*

A TASTE OF HOME

Photographer Anders Schønnemann
Styling Nathalie Schwer
Coffee mug HAY
Teapot, bowls and glass pitcher Broste
Cafetieres Georg Jensen
Scented candle Oliver Gustav
*Special thanks to Les Gens Heureux
for the location*

THE CLOUD APPRECIATION
SOCIETY

Photographer Maia Flore

KEEPING IT CIVIL
SIMPLE PHILOSOPHIES

Illustrator Katrin Coetzer

CULINARY ESSENTIALS

Illustrator Katrin Coetzer
*Special thanks to Stephanie Cmar
and Andre Chiang*

PASSEGGIATA

Photographer Tec Petaja

MY BEDSIDE TABLE:
THE FASHION DESIGNER

Photographer Anders Schønnemann
Styling Nathalie Schwer
*Special thanks to Les Gens
Heureux for the location*
*Special thanks to Sofia Bibliowicz
and Mode PR*

THE LUNCH BOX:
BREAD AND BUTTER

Photographers Gentl & Hyers
Special thanks to Edge Reps

THE BEST MEDICINE

Hair Aimee Hershan at Stella Creative
Makeup Victoria Bond at Caren
Retouching Oliver Carver
Casting Simon Lewis at Cast and Elect
Production We Are Up Production
Models Nadja at Elite Models London,
Genesis at Select Model Management,
Chen at Select Model Management,
Nyasha at Elite Models London, Cosmo
at Kids London Model Agency, Kofi at
AMCK Models, Nader at Elisabeth Smith
Agency, Tom at D1 Model Management
and Georgina at Models 1

Clothing
Page 37: Shirt by Joseph
Page 38: Dress by Antipodium
Page 39: Shirtdress by COS
Page 40: Jumpsuit by Raquel Allegra
Page 41: Sweatshirt by Designers Remix
at Selfridges
Page 42: Sweater by Jigsaw
Page 43: T-shirt by COS; trousers
by Carven
Page 44: Sweater by APC; trousers
by Our Legacy
Page 45: Shirtdress by COS
Page 46: Dress by COS
Page 47: Sweatshirt by Designers Remix
at Selfridges

A SENSE OF BELONGING
*Special thanks to Rokas Darulis at Saint
Luke, Damian Flack, Claudia Difra,
Eve Delf, Francis Lane, David Lamb,
Keyleen Nguyen, Rebecca Wordingham
at Saint Luke, Holly Moore, Cathy
Butterworth, Jose Quijano at D+V
Management and Prana Production*

**TICKLED PINK:
THE WATERMELON MENU**
Page 86: Plate and bowl Casalinga
Page 89: Green and white plate Casalinga
Page 90: Green bowls H. Skjalm P

**HOW TO BE AN ESSENTIALIST:
AN INTERVIEW WITH
GREG MCKEOWN**
Quote from Essentialism: The Disciplined
Pursuit of Less *by Greg McKeown. Copyright
2014 by Greg McKeown used by permission.
Published by Crown Business, an imprint
of the Crown Publishing Group, a division
of Random House LLC*

THE ESSENTIAL ENDEAVORS
*Special thanks to Rufus Knight, Daniel
Wikey, Megumi Iino, Mie Takamatsu,
Oki Sato, Pannawat Muangmoon, Tory
Holmes from Blade PR and Ignacio Mattos*

RECIPE: OLIVE OIL CAKE
*Special thanks to Chef Michael Anthony
Special thanks to Edge Reps*

HOME TOUR: NATURAL HABITAT
Styling & Production Helle Walsted

KINFOLK GATHERINGS
Styling (paper plate photo) Karen Mordechai
*Special thanks to Sunday Suppers Studio,
Brooklyn, New York. Thanks to our partners*
De Alma e Coração and Simply Sebastião

SPECIAL THANKS
*Thanks to Chantal Anderson, Stella
Berkofsky, Jesse Kamm, Grant Harder,
Abi Huynh, Thomas Lykke, Kenya Hara
and Lucini Italia*